Merv

Tus▲

Nishapur Mashhad

Balkh

URASAN

Herat

RAN

Qandahar

SISTAN

Kirman

KIRMAN

Bandar Abbas

MAKRAN

PERSIA: HISTORY AND HERITAGE

PERSIA

HISTORY and HERITAGE

Edited by

John A. BOYLE

HENRY MELLAND · LONDON

First published in Great Britain by
Henry Melland Limited,
23 Ridgmount Street, London WC1E 7AH, in 1978
distributed by
George Allen & Unwin (Publishers) Limited,
Ruskin House, 40 Museum Street, London WC1A 1LU

ISBN 0 9500730 2 4   Hardbacked edition
ISBN 0 9500730 3 2   Paperbacked edition

Set in Monotype Baskerville 169
and printed litho in Great Britain
by W & J Mackay Ltd, Chatham

Designed by William Fenton ARCA

Contents

Illustrations

Foreword

SIR ROGER STEVENS GCMG

British Ambassador to Persia 1954–58
Author of 'The Land of the Great Sophy'

Persia and Britain have looked at each other for a long time but more often than not through distorting mirrors; neither has viewed the other steadily or seen her whole.

The fluctuating fortunes of our two countries, with the fluctuations usually syncopated, are partly responsible. Consider the record. When Cyrus was creating, or for that matter when Alexander was destroying, the Persian Empire, we were Ancient Britons still staining ourselves with woad. The Persians, after succumbing to Alexander, withstood the Roman invasion; the British did not. Britain was progressively converted to Christianity over a period which covered the Arab invasion of Persia and the acceptance of Islam. While we were building Gothic cathedrals and our nobles were curbing the power of the monarchy, Persia was being overrun by Genghis Khan and Tamerlane. When Englishmen attracted by trade first came in any numbers to Persia, during Queen Elizabeth's reign, they were impressed by the splendours of Isfahan and the Safavid court. Persia continued relatively prosperous and stable while England was rent by civil war. When, a century later, following the Afghan invasion, Persia was plunged into prolonged disorder, a secure and confident Britain was forging an industrial revolution and laying the foundations of her Empire, including her Indian Empire next door to Persia. The 19th century saw Britain at the apex of her power and Persia at the nadir of her recent fortunes. Today, after two world wars, Britain is struggling with economic forces which she cannot fully control while Persia, borne up by similar forces, is on the way to achieving unprecedented prosperity.

Is it surprising that, against this kaleidoscopic background, our two countries have not always seen each other in true perspective?

Moreover, so far as British understanding of Persia is concerned, there have been other complicating factors. Should the country be called Persia or Iran? The two names seem to have acquired rather different connotations. Persia – as she is known in this book – does not fit easily into the sort of categorization to which modern man, with his urge to simplify everything, is prone. Persia is Asia, yet her people are Aryan, that is of European origin. She is in the Middle East, but not an Arab country. Her language is related to Sanskrit, yet is written in Arabic characters. She is an Islamic country but has a long, pre-Islamic tradition of monarchy. Unlike most oil-producing states of the Middle East, she has a substantial population and considerable economic resources other than oil. Though constantly invaded and often politically weak, Persia's language and her artistic achievements have profoundly influenced neighbouring countries, especially India. Her monuments, both from classical times and since the coming of Islam, bear witness to a distinctive and enduring civilization.

The British first learned about Persia's glorious past from the understandably critical pens of Greek and Roman historians; it was difficult to match this to their direct knowledge of the country, which for practical purposes only began in the 17th century. Their later experience of the country and its people stemmed largely from British India; Persia, then, was seen to have an interesting past but an unpromising future. The past is still there, but the future has been transformed and we, in this country, are more involved with it than we have ever been, or even dreamt of being, before.

It is a good time, therefore, to ask ourselves searching questions. How much, for instance, do we really understand or even know about Persia's past? May this throw some light on the present and the future?

For two centuries and more, British scholars and travellers have been fascinated by different aspects of Persian civilization – her long and momentous history, the beauty of Persian language and poetry, the art of Persian miniaturists, the skill and originality of her architects and designers, the glories of Persian carpets and pottery, the lessons to be learnt from the unending wealth of Persian archaeological sites. Despite all this, it is not easy for the ordinary layman, who today may find himself suddenly plunged, without much warning, into Persian affairs, to obtain a rapid but rewarding insight into the many facets of Persia's history and heritage which it is both desirable to understand and enjoyable to savour. For all those who have dealings with Persia – and their number has increased fantastically in the last ten years – this book will be of great value. In a series of chapters at once scholarly and readable, it provides a clear and well balanced summary of Persian history and helps the reader better to appreciate the significance of Persia's artistic achievements. Read it, and you will find that you have acquired a fuller understanding of a country and a people whose promising future is closely bound up with an exciting and eventful past.

Roger Stevens

Hill Farm
Thursley
Surrey
January 1978

The Authors

J. A. BOYLE

Professor Boyle is head of the Department of Persian Studies, University of Manchester. He is also a Member of the Governing Council of the British Institute of Persian Studies, and of the Editorial Board of the *Cambridge History of Iran*.

Editor of Volume V of the *Cambridge History*, to which he contributed the chapter on the Il-Khans of Persia, he is now editing Volume VI.

He is on the Advisory Board of the Tehran University journal *Iran-Shenasi*, and is also a Member of the Gibb Memorial Trust for the publication of Arabic, Persian and Turkish texts.

Professor Boyle was awarded the Order and Decoration of Sepass, First Class, by the Iranian Ministry of Education for his translation (1958) of the 13th century historian Juvaini's *History of the World-Conqueror*.

He edited, jointly with Professor Jahn of the University of Leiden, a Memorial Volume (1969) to celebrate the 650th anniversary of the death of the great Iranian statesman and historian Rashid al-Din.

Recent publications include translations of Rashid al Din under the title *The Successors of Genghis Khan* (1971) and of the Persian mystical poet 'Attar's narrative poem *Ilahi-nama* or 'Book of God' (1977).

LAURENCE LOCKHART

Dr Lockhart, who was born in 1890 and died in 1975, studied Persian and Arabic under the inspired teaching of Professor E. G. Browne at Cambridge. His finest and most well researched work of scholarship is thought by many to be his *Life of Nadir Shah*, published in 1938. He later continued his deep interest in 18th century Persian history with the *Fall of the Safavi Dynasty and the Afghan Occupation of Persia* (1958) which was regarded as an important contribution to Iranian history.

Besides these major historical studies Dr Lockhart wrote commentaries on Italian travellers to Persia in *Il Nuovo Ramusio* and articles for the new *Encyclopaedia of Islam*, besides numerous contributions to learned journals.

In *Cities of Destiny*, edited by Arnold Toynbee, Dr Lockhart wrote of 'Shah 'Abbas' Isfahan' – this beautiful old city being his favourite.

He was also a keen photographer and illustrated many of his own books, and also those of other authors.

Dr Lockhart was editor for many years of *Iran*, Journal of the British Institute of Persian Studies.

In all he devoted some sixty years of his life to Persian studies.

P. R. L. BROWN

Professor Brown obtained his BA at Oxford in 1956. Between then and 1974 he was a Fellow of All Souls; Reader in Late Roman and Early Byzantine History, University of Oxford; and Lecturer in Medieval History at Merton College. He became a Fellow of the British Academy in 1971 and is also an Hon D Theol, Fribourg.

He took up his present appointment as Professor of History and Head of Department, Royal Holloway College, University of London, in 1974.

Among his works in preparation for publication are 'The Sasanian Empire in the Near East' for the journal *Iran*; and *The Changing of the Kingdoms: society and culture in the Sasanian Empire and Byzantium 500 to 700 AD*.

Besides many other papers and lectures, he has also published *Augustine of Hippo: a biography* (1967); *Religion and Society in the Age of St Augustine* and *The World of Late Antiquity* (1971).

L. P. ELWELL-SUTTON

Professor of Persian, University of Edinburgh, since 1976, he is a BA London 1934 (1st class Arabic). He is a Member of the Royal Asiatic Society, the Royal Central Asian Society, the Iran Society and the British Association of Orientalists.

He lectured in Arabic at the School of Oriental and African Studies, London University, 1939–40; in Persian at the University of Edinburgh, 1952–60, becoming Senior Lecturer in 1960 until 1969 and then Reader from 1969–76.

Professor Elwell-Sutton joined the Anglo-Iranian Oil Company, Iran, in 1935 until 1938. He served with the Ministry of Information in 1939 and the BBC Near Eastern Services from 1940–43 and from 1948–52. The years between (1943–47) were spent with the British Embassy in Tehran. He was Chairman of the British Association of Orientalists during 1971–72.

Publications: *Colloquial Persian* (1941, 7th edn 1966); *Modern Iran* (1941, 4th edn 1944); *The Wonderful Seahorse and other Persian Tales* (1950); *Guide to Iranian Area Study* (1952); *Persian Proverbs* (1954); *Persian Oil: A Study in Power Politics* (1955); *Elementary Persian Grammar* (1963, 3rd edn 1972); *The Persian Metres* (1976); *The Horoscope of Asadullah Mirza* (1977); translations of *Rahnema: Payambar, the Prophet* (1964–66, 2nd edn 1971); *Ali Dashti: In Search of Omar Khayyam* (1971).

P. W. AVERY

Peter Avery was born in 1923 and came to the Persian language during naval service in the Indian Ocean in the Second World War. His main ambition was to read Persian poetry in the original, but he has also realized that while a country's history cannot be understood without a knowledge of its literature, especially when it is a literature like that of Iran, the poetry cannot be fully understood without some acquaintance with the historical environment in which the poets lived. Mr Avery graduated in Persian from London in 1949 and is now Lecturer in Persian Studies in the Faculty of Oriental Studies and a Fellow of King's College at Cambridge.

B. W. ROBINSON

Mr Robinson was educated at Winchester College (Exhibitioner) from 1926–31 and at Corpus Christi College, Oxford (BA 1935; MA, B Litt 1938). He read Classics (Mods and Greats) then wrote a B Litt thesis on Persian Painting in the Bodleian Library. He developed a keen interest in Persian painting from the age of eight or nine. After a short spell of teaching he entered the Victoria and Albert Museum in January 1939, at first in the Library and then in the Department of Metalwork. He became Deputy Keeper in 1954, Keeper in 1966 and Keeper Emeritus in 1972, retiring in July 1976. His war service was spent with the Royal Sussex Regiment, 2nd Punjab Regiment (Indian Army) in India, Burma and Malaya 1941–46. He was President of the Royal Asiatic Society 1970–73.

Mr Robinson is the author of a number of books, articles and reviews on Persian painting, Japanese colour-prints and Japanese swords, from 1948. His books include catalogues of Persian paintings in the Bodleian Library (1958), the Chester Beatty Library (part-author, 1960–62), the India Office Library (1976) and the Keir Collection (1976). He has also published a monograph on the Japanese artist Kuniyoshi (1961) and *The Arts of the Japanese Sword* (1961, 2nd edn 1972). He is at present working on a catalogue of the Persian paintings in the John Rylands Library, Manchester.

He organized and staged two loan exhibitions of Persian painting (1951–52 and 1967) and a centenary exhibition of the works of Kuniyoshi (1961) at the Victoria and Albert Museum.

D. N. WILBER

Dr Wilber studied at Princeton University and received his PhD from that Institution. Trained as an architect, he was first a member of several archaeological excavations in the Middle East and then made a series of tours of architectural exploration in Iran.

Residence in Iran during the Second World War resulted in diverting his attention and concern to the modern Middle East. During many years in which he served as a consultant to public agencies and private concerns, he made frequent trips throughout the region, and found time to pursue independent research.

From among his books those on Iran include *Persepolis. The Archaeology of Parsa. Seat of the Persian Kings; Persian Gardens and Garden Pavilions; The Architecture of Islamic Iran: The Il-Khanid Period; Contemporary Iran; Iran Past and Present;* and *Riza Shah Pahlavi: The Resurrection and Reconstruction of Iran.*

R. H. PINDER-WILSON

Mr Pinder-Wilson was educated at Westminster and Christ Church, Oxford. He served in the British Museum from 1949–76, where he was in charge of the Islamic Antiquities, and is now Director of the British Institute of Afghan Studies, Kabul.

His publications include *Islamic Art* (London, 1957); *Persian Painting of the Fifteenth Century* (London, 1958); *Paintings from Islamic Lands* (ed London 1969).

G. WILFRID SEAGER

Mr Seager's connection with the East went back to the death of his great-grandfather at Balaklava, his grandfather working as a young man helping Florence Nightingale at her hospital at Scutari. Mr Seager's father and he himself were both born in Bebek, a village on the Bosphorus where a small British community had made their home, carrying on import/export and shipping business between Turkey and Great Britain.

After returning from school in England, he was sent to Kirman in South Persia in the employ of The Oriental Carpet Manufacturers Limited, a British company which supervised the production and world-wide distribution of hand-made oriental carpets and rugs.

He joined the Intelligence Corps in the Second World War and was transferred to the Ministry of Information, which sent him to Tehran where he became First Secretary and Director of Public Relations at the British Embassy, a post he held until 1947 when he returned to London as Joint Managing Director of OCM (London) Limited and remained there until his retirement in December 1966.

After retirement Mr Seager maintained his close interest in Persia, particularly by promoting friendship between Great Britain and Persia through the Iran Society as Honorary Treasurer, Honorary Secretary and then for thirteen years as Chairman, being made a Vice-President upon relinquishing that position.

In recognition of these services he was awarded the Honour of the Order of Humayun by the Persian Government.

1

Persia through the Ages

The Beginnings: the Achaemenids

LAURENCE LOCKHART AND J. A. BOYLE

Few countries can rival Iran in the length and the variety of her history. One has only to look at a map of the Middle East to see why this history has been so eventful. The country is situated for the most part between the depressions of the Caspian Sea and the Persian Gulf and its territory has, therefore, often served in the past as a bridge for peoples and tribes migrating westwards from the vast areas of central Asia and beyond, and sometimes in the reverse direction.

We know as yet little regarding the early peoples of this very ancient land. They were neither Aryan nor Semitic and, for want of a better label, they have been called either Caspian or Caucasian. These peoples were for the most part cave-dwellers who earned their livelihood by hunting. Their aggregate numbers were undoubtedly low, for no country can support large numbers of people who subsist solely on the game they can kill (one person per square mile is about the limit for subsistence).

It was only after the introduction of agriculture and the domestication of animals – two innovations of great importance – that a change occurred in the way of life of these peoples. They became settled on the land and, although they may still have continued to hunt, this activity was on a decreasing scale. Handicrafts were evolved and by degrees wonderful proficiency was attained, as is exemplified by the finds of archaeologists in various parts of the country. Naturally enough, these handicrafts became more varied and exhibited still greater skill after the use of metals had been discovered. The finds by, for example, Professor Negahban, at Marlik, in Gilan, show that a marvellous proficiency had been attained by the end of the second millennium or early in the first millennium BC.

Early centres of civilization were at Siyalk (adjacent to modern Kashan) and, slightly later, at Susa, destined to be for a time one of the great cities of the world.

The Elamites were the first of the peoples of Persia to emerge from the darkness of antiquity into the light – at first only dim and fitful – of the early historic period. While some inhabited the mountainous areas of south-west Persia, others settled in the plains of what is now Khuzistan. They were skilled craftsmen and in due course they evolved a pictographic script, which was later replaced by the cuneiform system which they borrowed from the Assyrians. They were very warlike people, as is shown by their destruction of Siyalk and, in later times, their long struggles with the Assyrians.

The first Aryan entry into Persia occurred about halfway through the second millennium BC. It seems to have left little or no mark on the Elamites, but the Kassites, the Elamites' northern neighbours, came under Aryan influence. This influence is shown not only by their adoption of the horse, but also by the subsequent hybrid nature of their religious system in which Kassite and Babylonian deities subsisted side by side with Indo-European gods such as Buriash (the Greek Boreas), the god of the north wind.

While, except among the Kassites, the first Aryan or Indo-European irruption into Persia had little effect upon its peoples, the second Aryan influx, which took place some five centuries later, had consequences which were not only widespread, but were also of fundamental importance. The second batch of Aryans acquired in due course the cultures and skills of the original inhabitants. Little by little a new race, predominantly Aryan in character and speech, was evolved; this race was destined to make history on a hitherto quite unprecedented scale. These Aryans were the tribes of the Medes and Persians. They were kindred peoples, as was shown by the similarity of their languages and ways.

It is through the Assyrian records that we first hear of the Medes and Persians. Shalmaneser III, when quelling a revolt in the Zagros mountain region to the east of his country, in 836BC came into contact with the Persian chiefs of Parsua and made them pay tribute. Parsua was then the name given to the region to the west of Lake Urmiya (now Rezaieh) where the Persians had settled.[1] Shalmaneser subsequently marched south-eastwards and subjugated the Medes.

It is clear that when the Medes and Persians first emerged from obscurity, they were not as yet at all powerful. Had it not been for the intervention of the Urartians, a warlike and formidable people who inhabited what is now part of north-western Iran and also of what are now the Turkish districts of Van and Ararat (in fact, the name 'Ararat' is derived from 'Urartu'), the Assyrians would have completely subjugated them.

In 670BC the Assyrian records refer to a Median chieftain named Khshathrita (he was also called Fravartish, 'Protector', hence Herodotus's 'Phraortes'), who was a fierce opponent of the Assyrians. He was the ruler of Akessaia, a town which had been the capital of the Kassites and which the Medes were soon to rename Hagmatana (Ecbatana, the present Hamadan). By this time the Kassites and the Medes had to a large extent become assimilated.

Before attacking the Assyrians, Khshathrita invaded the area held by the Persians and made their ruler Teispes (Chishpish) his vassal. This Teispes was the son of Hakhamanish (Achaemenes), the eponym of the royal line of the Persians. Khshathrita, though he failed in his struggle with the Assyrians, may justly be regarded as the founder of the Median kingdom. He met his end in battle with the Scythians, a fierce and warlike Aryan tribe who lived by rapine. Khshathrita was succeeded by his son Cyaxeres (Uvakhshatara) in 653BC, but he was soon afterwards assailed by the Scythians who for twenty-eight years enforced their rule on him and his people.

This long period of Scythian rule was ended when Cyaxeres, having made their leaders drink to excess at a banquet, had them all slain. The Scythians then sought to avenge their slaughtered chiefs, but they were eventually overcome. Irksome though it had been, this period of servitude under the Scythians had certain advantages for the Medes, for they learnt the use of the bow. Furthermore, it was probably from the Scythians that they became, like them, notable exponents of mobility in warfare.

Meanwhile, Teispes, the King of the Persians, had taken advantage of the temporary eclipse of the Medes by the Scythians, to free himself from the shackles

[1] Subsequently this name was given to two other regions as the Persians moved south, the last to have this name being the Persis of the Greeks and the Pars or Fars of modern times.

imposed by the former. Elam by this time was on the decline, and he was able to move southwards from his land of Parsumash and annex Parsa, the modern Pars or Fars, and Anshan. He divided his realm between his two sons Ariaramnes and Cyrus I; Ariaramnes proclaimed himself as 'the great king, king of kings, king of the land of Parsa'. A golden tablet found at Hamadan, besides bearing Ariaramnes's titles states:

'This land of the Persians which I possess, provided with fine horses and good men, it is the great god Ahura Mazda who has given it to me. I am the king of this land.'

As Professor Ghirshman has stated,[1] this tablet is the oldest Achaemenian object known and bears the earliest known text of the Old Persian language. Also discovered at Hamadan was a golden tablet bearing a similar inscription, but with the name of Ariaramnes's successor Arsames. Arsames, however, did not for long enjoy the possession of the throne, for he was soon defeated and deposed by the Median king Cyaxeres. The latter, in the meanwhile, had, in alliance with the Babylonians, overwhelmed the dreaded Assyrians and had sacked and destroyed their capital Nineveh. Though triumphant over the Persians, Cyaxeres allowed members of the Achaemenid family to govern their territories under his suzerainty. The Achaemenid Cambyses I, the King of Parsumash and adjacent lands, married the daughter of Astyages, Cyaxeres's son. From this union was born Cyrus, who in due course became ruler of the Achaemenid lands in south-western Persia as a vassal of the Median king.

The history of the Achaemenid Empire is closely linked with that of Greece; and apart from inscriptions and the archaeological evidence, our main, and in some cases our only, authorities are the great Greek historians Herodotus, Thucydides and Xenophon. The names of Cyrus, Cambyses, Darius, Xerxes and Artaxerxes are therefore as familiar to us as those of their Greek contemporaries. The history of Cyrus is related at length by Herodotus: his revolt against the Medes and conquest of their empire; his war against Croesus of Lydia which brought under his sway the whole of western Asia Minor from the Halys (the modern Kizil Irmak) to the Greek cities on the Mediterranean coast; the conquest of Babylon with the consequent accession of Syria, Palestine and Phoenicia, and finally his death in battle against the Massagetae, an Iranian tribe that still pursued the old nomadic

[1] R. Ghirshman, *Iran from the Earliest Times to the Islamic Conquest*, London, 1954, p 120.

life of the Aryans in the region beyond the Jaxartes or Sir Darya in what is now Soviet Central Asia. After the fall of Babylon, as we may read in the Bible, he made a proclamation that the Temple of Jehovah in Jerusalem should be rebuilt at his expense and he gave permission to the Jewish exiles to return to their homeland. It was acts like these and his humane treatment of conquered kings and peoples, contrasting with the cruelty shown in such circumstances by his Assyrian and Babylonian predecessors, that prompted Xenophon in his *Cyropedia* or 'Education of Cyrus' to hold him up as the model of an ideal monarch.

It was Cyrus's son Cambyses who conquered Egypt, which was to remain part of the Persian Empire for nearly 200 years. With the death of Cambyses the succession passed into another branch of the Achaemenid family in the person of Darius I or Darius the Great, under whom the Empire reached its widest expansion: in the famous rock inscription at Bisutun near Kermanshah he enumerates 'the lands of which I hold possession beyond Persis (*ie* Fars), over which I held sway, which brought me tribute, which did that which was commanded them by me, and wherein my Law was maintained: Media, Susiana (*ie* Elam), Parthia, Haraiva (Herat), Bactria, Sughd, Chorasmia, Drangiana, Arachosia, Thattagush (probably the Punjab), India, Egypt, Armenia, Cappadocia, Sparda (Sardis), the Ionians, *etc etc*.' These territories he divided into 20 provinces, over each of which he set a *khshatrapa*, a word which we know in its Greek form *satrap*. Darius was a great builder: it was he who designed the famous platform-palace of Persepolis, the ruins of which figured so largely in the recent celebrations. The building of a palace at Susa, whither he removed his capital from Babylon, is described in one of his inscriptions, which shows how workmen were recruited and materials imported from every corner of his empire: 'This is the palace which I built at Susa. From afar its ornamentation was brought. Downward the earth was dug until I reached the rock in the earth. When the excavation was made, then rubble was packed down, the Babylonian people they did (these tasks). The cedar timber, this – a mountain by name Lebanon – from there it was brought; the Assyrian people, they brought it to Babylon, from Babylon the Carians and Ionians brought it to Susa. The *yaka* timber was brought from Gandara and from Carmania. The gold was brought from Sardis and from Bactria, which was wrought here. The precious stones lapis lazuli and cornelian which were wrought here, these were brought from

Sogdiana. The precious stone turquoise this was brought from Egypt. The ornament-
ation with which the wall was adorned, that was brought from Ionia. The ivory
which was wrought here was brought from Ethiopia and from Sind and from
Arachosia. The stone columns were wrought here – a village by name Abiradus in
Elam – from there they were brought. The stone-cutters who wrought the stone,
these were Ionians and Sardians. The goldsmiths who wrought the gold, these were
Medes and Egyptians. The men who wrought the baked bricks these were
Babylonians. The men who adorned the all, these were Medes and Egyptians.'

Darius, it should be noted was also the most notable upholder of the worship of
Ahura Mazda, one of the ancient pagan hierarchy of deities who, as a result of the
reforms of Zoroaster (of unknown date, but probably many centuries before the
period of which we are now speaking), had become the supreme God of the mono-
theistic Iranian faith. In his inscriptions Ahura Mazda is the only deity named;
later on other figures in the pantheon – Mithra, Anahita, Arta – reappear.

The war against Greece begun by Darius was continued by his son Xerxes; but
the defeat of the Persians at Marathon, the heroic stand of the Spartans at
Thermopylae and the naval battle off Salamis belong rather to European than
to Asian history and require no mention here. Seventy years later, when Xenophon
took part in the ill-fated expedition of Cyrus the Younger against his brother
Artaxerxes II, he was plainly impressed by the vastness, strength and solidity that
still distinguished the Achaemenid Empire, of which his *Anabasis* supplies so vivid a
picture. Artaxerxes III, who ascended the throne in 359BC was the last of the great
Achaemenids: he restored Egypt to the Persian Empire, which was however
destined soon to be lost by his successor Darius III to Alexander the Great. The
victories of Alexander and the Greco-Persian Empire of his successors the Seleucids
do not concern us here. Alexander's name is known throughout Asia, not because
of his real exploits, but because of the legends of the Alexander Romance or Pseudo-
Callisthenes which penetrated as far as Mongolia. In the Persian National Epic
he is made out to be the son not of Philip of Macedon, but of the contemporary
Persian monarch by Philip's daughter, whom he had divorced and sent back to her
father, who, wishing to conceal the slight to his daughter, pretended that Alexander
was his son by one of his own wives. This is the later tradition. In an older and
more authentic tradition he is represented as 'the accursed Alexander the Roman,

who urged on by the evil spirit brought havoc, destruction and slaughter into Persia, burned Persepolis and the Zoroastrian scriptures . . . and finally self-destroyed fled to hell'.

Parthians and Sasanians

P. R. L. BROWN

A century and a half after the death of Alexander, a Greek historian, Polybius, could write: 'I ask you, do you think that either the Persians and the Persian ruler or the Macedonians and their king . . . could ever have believed that at the time when we live the very name of the Persians would have perished utterly – those who were the masters of the whole world?'

Polybius, of course, was referring to the end of the Achaemenid Empire, which had riveted the attention of the world. The five centuries which elapsed between its fall and the establishment of an Empire of comparable size and stability – the Sasanian dynasty, founded by Ardashir I (AD208–240) – seem an anti-climax. But this is only so for those who wish history to consist of the formation of grandiose Empires and the emergence of strong 'national' states with firm frontiers. Life in the ancient world had room for more than that. Instead, we have a period of 'low profile' political institutions under whose protection the diverse and cosmopolitan culture of the area between Central Asia and the Euphrates continued to evolve with undiminished vigour.

The direct successors of Alexander – the Seleucids (named from Alexander's general, Seleucus) – turned their back on the Iranian plateau. Their city, Seleucia, on the Tigris, looked westwards to Syria, just as, in later centuries, the cities that grew up within a few miles of it – first, Ctesiphon and then Baghdad – spoke of a commitment to Mesopotamia and of ambition to the Mediterranean. The cities of the plateau, Susa and Ecbatana, became backwaters, and traditional Iran, a political vacuum.

Yet, further to the east, the Greek settlers of Khurasan and Central Asia fared differently. Like many colonists who feel a long way from home, they remained for generations more Greek than the Greeks. They collaborated with the native populations of Central Asia to preserve and expand the economic life of the oasis-cities: forty-five thousand square kilometres of land (three times the amount now under cultivation) were brought under irrigation around the Oxus and the Iaxartes (Amu-Darya and Syr-Darya). Native and Greek lived easily side by side. Excavations at Nysa (Turkmeniya SSR) reveal a perfect Greek theatre: yet the documents of the administration were in the old Aramaic of the Achaemenid Empire, and beneath the haunting classical perfection of a copy of the Venus of Milo we can detect the features of a local girl.

Around these colonists and their local allies stretched six hundred thousand square kilometres of desert steppe – the world of the pastoral nomads. It is from this steppe that the next 'strong men' of Persian history came: the Parthians, who had lived east of the Caspian Sea. They slowly infiltrated, rather than conquered, the Greek settlements of Eastern Iran. The Parthian king, Mithridates (170–138BC) established their Empire over traditional Iran. In 53BC (only two years after Julius Caesar had routed the half-naked Britons) the self-confident Roman world was stunned by the utter defeat of the Roman legions – forty thousand men in all – and the death of their general, Crassus, at the hands of the half-known Parthians. At the battle of Carrhae (Harran) in Northern Mesopotamia, Parthian cavalry, trained on the steppes of Central Asia, baffled and then crushed the legions. Heavily armoured horsemen (human tanks, like medieval knights) broke the infantry formations; and the light cavalry 'mopped up' the rest by deadly arrow-fire from horseback – the famous 'Parthian shot'.

Yet the Parthians did not wish to be either conquerors or Empire builders. Their cavalry was most at home in Iran and Central Asia. Their political structure was lax. The Parthian kings came increasingly to depend on the loyalty of the great families of Iran. These would fight for them at the head of their own private armies. The Parthian army and the state was closer, in its traditions of 'soft' government and in its dependence on the loyalty of hereditary great families, to the 'feudalism' that modern Western historians associate with the Western Middle Ages.

It is, however, a Western prejudice to be interested only in this aspect of Parthian rule. The Parthians saw themselves as the protectors, even as the 'impresarios', of the rich and manifold cultures they had taken over. Enclaves of Greek culture continued to flourish. In the Near East, Greek-style coins and Greek-style edicts were part of the 'shop window' of respectable rule. Parthian rulers continued this. There was a grim streak in their Hellenism: at a command performance of the *Bacchae* of Euripides, it was the head of the defeated Roman general, Crassus, that served as the 'stage prop' for the torn off head of Pentheus in the grisly climax of the drama.

Other cultures continued to flourish under their 'soft' government. Architectural innovations of the greatest importance for the future development of building in Iran can be traced back to this period: the dome resting in a square through the use of the squinch was among these. In the late Parthian site of Qaleh-i Yazdgird, perched on a ledge of the Zagros mountains above Qasr-i Shirin, stucco-work that is an exquisite fusion of Greek and ancient Iranian motifs has been discovered on a plateau ringed by high walls. The embattled site – the residence of some as yet unknown king or nobleman – combined with the amazing craftsmanship of its decoration is a symbol of the rich contradictions of Parthian rule.

By contrast, the Sasanian Empire emerged from the heart of old Iran – from Fars. Ardashir I (AD208–240) and his son, Shapur I (AD240–272) immediately gave it a distinctive, almost monolithic, profile. In AD224 Ardashir defeated the last Parthian monarch, Artavan V; in AD226 he entered Ctesiphon, in Mesopotamia, and took the title of King of Kings. In the rock-carvings of Naqsh-i Rustam and Firuzabad, Ardashir holds the centre of the stage: on horseback, he topples his enemies with his lance; in a magnificent, quiet gesture, he receives the 'Ring of Empire' from the God of the traditional Zoroastrian faith, Ahura Mazda. His son, Shapur I was a conqueror: in three great campaigns – in AD 252, 257 and again in 260 – he marched through the Roman Near East, capturing the Emperor Valerian in person.

The rock carvings at Naqsh-i Rustam and Bishapur told the story to every passer-by: 'And Valerian the Caesar came towards us with an army of seven hundred thousand men . . . and we took him with our own hand . . . and the provinces of Syria, Cilicia and Cappadocia, we burnt, ravaged and conquered, taking their inhabitants captive.'

Following Near Eastern practice, these captives were settled in Iran, to form the nucleus for new cities, with new industries. Silk-weaving, hydraulic engineering, and the translation of Greek medical works by re-settled families were connected with the foundation by Shapur I of Bishapur and Gundeshapur.

Ardashir, Shapur and their successors, considered themselves as enjoying the support of the traditional religion of Iran – at least, of *their* Iran, the province of Fars: Zoroastrianism. The Zoroastrian clergy emerged with a 'high' profile. They were organized as a hierarchy under a high-priest who collaborated intimately with the King of Kings. The Magi, therefore, came to act as religious judges throughout the provinces; and the fire-temples were centres both of worship and of loyalty to the Sasanian Empire.

Yet the Sasanians, in replacing the Parthians, inherited their problems. These remained formidable.

First and foremost: distance. It took over two months to reach the capital of Ctesiphon from the mountains of Armenia. Eastern Iran, with its dangerous frontier with the nomads of Central Asia, was almost another world. The King of Kings had to be a *diraz-dast* – a man 'with a long hand'. The success of the Sasanian rulers of the 3rd and 4th centuries in overcoming distance was amazing. Shapur II (309–379) battered the frontiers of the Roman Empire in northern Mesopotamia for fifteen years. In 363 he lured the Emperor Julian and his army to total disaster. Yet, in between these campaigns, he held the frontiers of the Caucasus and of Central Asia against the nomads. These nomads he would 'syphon off' into his army, bringing to his campaigns in Mesopotamia skills in cavalry warfare learnt in the hard school of the steppes of the Caspian.

Second: the Sasanians ruled a variety of peoples and cultures. They had to maintain traditions of 'soft' government. This was less easy as religious intolerance replaced the easy going polytheism of Parthian times. In the 2nd century BC, a statue of Hercules could be carved, at Bisutun, on the same rock as bore inscriptions in honour of Ahura Mazda. In the 3rd and 4th centuries AD, the exclusiveness of the reformed Zoroastrian clergy met its match in the strong Christian communities established in Northern Syria, Armenia and Mesopotamia. Despite spasmodic clashes, the Sasanians made little attempt to absorb their religious minorities. As long as the Iranian upper-classes maintained their identity by adhering to a strict Zoroastrian orthodoxy, the non-Iranian subjects of the King of Kings could go their own way.

Distance, the threat of the nomads, religious ferment: these were problems that could never be solved forever. Under Firuz (459–484) disaster came. He died with his army fighting the Hephthalite nomad confederacy in Dehistan (Gurgan) in 484. Mazdak, a radical Zoroastrian, claimed to bring the people back to the true religion of Ahura Mazda by recreating Iranian society: the traditional great families were threatened, their grain stores looted in times of famine, their wives redistributed (this last was a primitive form of 'trust-breaking', to prevent the accumulation of great wealth through the intermarriage of great families).

Khusro I (531–579) Anoshirwan owed his position to having solved these problems with gusto. Mazdak and his followers were massacred. Royal power was re-established around an efficient court at Ctesiphon. The great audience hall of Khusro I – the *Ivan-i Khusro*, which captured the imagination of all later generations of Persians and Arabs – still stands outside Baghdad as a monument to his success. The 'long hand' of the King of Kings would reach out to punish injustice, and to bring in the taxes by means of a more flexible system, based on money-payments rather than on an annual division of the harvest. In 540 he sacked Antioch. Between 562 and 568 he broke the Hephthalite confederacy in a series of bitter campaigns. This was his real triumph. His coins proclaimed: 'Delivering Iran from fear.'

Under Khusro I, the Sasanian Empire could stand at the cross-roads of Asia. Excavations at Siraf on the Persian Gulf have revealed a well-established Persian maritime trade which, at that time, reached as far as Indonesia. The silk routes of Central Asia were in Persian hands. After the Arab conquest, Persian noblemen took this route to find safety and new careers: as cavalry generals, in the 8th century AD, they guarded the Great Wall of China as they had once guarded the great oasis-city of Merv. Cultural wealth flowed to the court of Khusro I. The doctor, Burzoe, travelled to India, bringing back translations of Indian legends and Indian works on embryology. Syrian Christians, who felt at ease in a tolerant court, translated the Greek medical works of Galen and wrote text-books of Greek logic. It is not surprising that the last philosophers of Athens, persecuted as pagans by the the Christian government of East Rome, should have stayed for a time at the court of Khusro I in 529.

Khusro I was the ideal ruler for the Sasanian state – always on the move, capable of patronising the widely-different groups within his Empire, deliberately maintaining, at Ctesiphon, a court larger than life. He is shown on a cameo: a bearded figure, with flowing hair, wearing a great winged crown and clasping a long sword between his knees – at one and the same time, a symbol of majesty and active warrior. Khusro II (591–628) his grandson was a more complex character. He was called *Abharvez* (Parviz) – Victorious. For a generation, he re-established the Empire of the Achaemenids in its full extent throughout the Near East: Antioch fell in 613, Egypt in 619, by 620 Persian armies had again reached the Bosphorus.

Yet he may have embarked on his conquests to avoid the problems of day-to-day government within his own Empire. For Khusro II failed to be a *diraz-dast* in the old style. His court had grown in size. Only the rich land of Iraq could support it in the winter, and the hill country of Western Kurdistan in the summer. He was tied to one place by his own magnificence, and was drawn increasingly to the West by his own success.

Unlike Khusro I, he could not make his presence felt on the Iranian plateau and along the frontiers of Central Asia. At the end of his reign, even Iraq crumbled. When the Arab raiders first entered Mesopotamia, they found a country decimated by plague, with its irrigation dams broken. Once the Arabs defeated the Persian army at the battle of Qadisiya, in 637, and had entered Ctesiphon, the last King of Kings Yazdgird III (632–651) found himself with nowhere to go. As the Parthians had done, some nine centuries earlier, the Arab horsemen found a political vacuum in Iran.

Yet, a landscape is stronger than any Empire. The Arabs were slower to absorb the plateau of Iran than any other region that they conquered. For centuries, small courts, who nourished memories of the grandeur of the Sasanians, survived in the mountains around the Caspian. In central Iran, Zoroastrian communities remained strong until the 13th century. The ideal of the rule of a just king, ordained by God, remained deeply rooted. And, beneath this ideal, there lay a stubborn faith, summed up in the religion of Zoroaster, that a settled, civilized life was something that had to be fought for – that what the Zoroastrians called 'the good things of

Ahura Mazda' (water, cattle, peaceable villages and good women: not merely grandiose Empires, but a just society) needed to be preserved and increased in a harsh land:

'The Empire will prosper, the common people will be freed from fear and will enjoy a good life. Science will advance, culture will be looked after, good manners will be further refined and men will be generous, just and gracious.'

From the Islamic Conquest to the Qajars

LAURENCE LOCKHART AND J. A. BOYLE

The triumph of the Muslim Arabs over the Sasanian Empire was due to two main causes. First, there was the exhaustion of the Sasanian power by the long-drawn-out struggle with the Byzantine Empire. Secondly, the Arabs were united as they had never been before by their new faith. The Arab conquest resulted, *inter alia*, in the disappearance of the Pahlavi language and, except in the more remote areas, of the Zoroastrian religion. Furthermore, the rigid monarchical system of the Sasanians was replaced by a democratic form of government under the Caliphate.

For many years the Persian people seemed to be eclipsed, yet beneath the surface they soon began to make their influence felt. Though the Arabic language became the chief literary medium, after a time there were many gifted Persians who achieved fame by their writings in that language. A development destined to be of great importance in later times was the adhesion of many Persians to the cause of the Shi'a or 'Party' of 'Ali, the Prophet Muhammad's son-in-law.[1] One of the strong reasons for this development was the belief among the the Persian Shi'a that Husain, the younger son of 'Ali and the Prophet's daughter Fatima, had married Shahribanu, the daughter of Yazdgird III, the last of the Sasanians.

In subsequent years, when the Umaiyad Caliphate became unpopular, many Persians supported the claims of the rival House of 'Abbas. A considerable part in the overthrow of the Umaiyads was played by a Persian named Abu Muslim.

In the 9th century AD, when the 'Abbasid Caliphate had lost some of its power and influence in outlying parts of its realm, the Persian spirit showed signs of resurgence by the appearance of local dynasties such as that of the Saffarids in 867,

---

[1] In the eyes of the Shi'a, 'Ali should have succeeded Muhammad on the latter's death, in place of Abu Bakr. They looked upon Abu Bakr, 'Umar and 'Uthman as interlopers.

31

the Samanids in 874 and the Buyids in 932. More or less simultaneously, the Persian language began to emerge, but in a new guise, as it was enriched by the inclusion of many Arabic words and it used the Arabic script in place of the cumbrous and difficult Pahlavi system of writing.

At their court at Bukhara, the enlightened Samanid rulers patronised men of great learning such as the famous philosopher Abu ʿAli ibn Sina (Avicenna). By means of lavish rewards they sought to attract to their courts poets and artists from Baghdad, and opened up schools and universities to compete with those in that city. Moreover, modern Persian literature may be said to have originated there, with the emergence of the poets Rudaki and Daqiqi.

So far, the Persian revival had been in the eastern and north-eastern parts of the country, but towards the end of the first quarter of the 10th century Mardavij ibn Ziyar seized power in the mountainous country to the south of the Caspian Sea. Apart from Mardavij, the most notable of the Ziyarids was his descendant Qabus ibn Vashmgir, who was a poet and a patron of poets. Qabus is famous for his remarkable tomb-tower, the Gunbad-i Qabus, in north-eastern Persia.

Another and more remarkable Persian dynasty arose in the Dailamite country just to the west of the territory of the Ziyarids. This was the dynasty founded by ʿAli, Hasan and Ahmad, the three sons of Abu Shujaʿ Buya. While ʿAli established himself in Fars, Hasan gained control over Persian Iraq. The third son Ahmad made himself master of Baghdad. Ahmad was a Shiʿi, but he did not deem himself to be sufficiently powerful to depose the weak ʿAbbasid Caliph al-Taʿiʿ and rule in his stead; however he held all the temporal power of the Caliphate in his hands. The best known and most illustrious of the Buyids was Fana-Khusrau, who reigned from 949 to 983. Like his forbears, he claimed descent from the Sasanians, and he was the first ruler in Islamic Persia to take the title *Shahanshah* ('King of Kings'). From the Caliph he received the title of ʿAzud al-Dauleh ('Supporting Arm of the

ABOVE
Palace of Cyrus the Great at Pasargadae
Collection of L. P. Elwell-Sutton

BELOW
Tomb of Cyrus the Great at Pasargadae
Collection of L. P. Elwell-Sutton

State'). 'Azud al-Dauleh kept his court at Shiraz, but he was often at Baghdad, which he did much to beautify by the erection of new buildings. Like the Sasanians, 'Azud al-Dauleh furthered irrigation by the construction of dams and irrigation canals in Persia and Mesopotamia. The most famous of his barrages is the Band-i Amir, over the Kur river, fifty miles to the north of Shiraz.

A new power soon arose in the east of Iran. This was the state ruled over by Mahmud of Ghazneh. He soon overthrew the Samanids and the Ziyarids, and he then displaced the Buyids of Persian Iraq (the Buyids of Mesopotamia, while they escaped this fate, were subsequently overthrown by the Seljuq conqueror Toghril Beg in 1055).

Mahmud sought to establish himself as a patron of learned men, a number of whom he gathered together at his court. One of those whom he patronized was Abu'l-Qasim Mansur Firdausi. Although he had begun his masterpiece the *Shahnameh* ('Book of Kings') under the Samanids, he completed it while Mahmud was on the throne. This work has contributed more than any other to the moulding of Persian national consciousness: in it Firdausi has preserved for all time the myths, legends and traditions of pre-Islamic Iran.

With the advent of the Ghuzz Turks under their leader Toghril Beg, Persia entered upon a new era. In successive stages, Toghril Beg defeated the Ghaznavids and seized their territories. By the overthrow of Khusrau Firuz, the Buyid ruler of Mesopotamia, he gained control over the feeble Caliph al-Qa'im, who hailed the conqueror as 'King of the East and West'.

The reigns of Toghril Beg (1037–63), his nephew and successor Alp Arslan (1063–72) and Malik-Shah (1072–92), Alp Arslan's son, covered the most brilliant period of Seljuq[1] rule over Persia. As Turkish reinforcements poured in, the Seljuqs were able greatly to extend their realm until it comprised most of western Asia.

[1] The term 'Seljuq' is derived from the man of that name who was Toghril's grandfather.

ABOVE
General view of Persepolis
Collection of L. P. Elwell-Sutton

BELOW
Frieze of tribute-bearers at Persepolis
Collection of L. P. Elwell-Sutton

Malik-Shah, who made Isfahan his capital, adorned it with the magnificent Masjid-i Jami' or Friday Mosque, and a number of other buildings. The government of Malik-Shah's vast realm was in the hands of his capable Vizier, Nizam al-Mulk. This famous minister, besides strengthening the royal authority, took steps to combat the propaganda and activities of the Isma'ilis and their sinister offshoot, the Order of the Assassins. It was at the hands of a *fida'i* or devotee of the Assassins that he met his end in 1092. Though he did so much to strengthen the Seljuq state, he also sowed the seeds of future weakness by his institution of the military governors known as Atabegs ('Father Lords') in various parts of the realm.

The Seljuq era, especially during the reign of Malik-Shah, was a great one for literature, science and religion. The famous mystic and theologian Ghazzali was a protégé of Nizam al-Mulk. Another notable figure was Omar Khayyam, the well-known mathematician, astronomer and philosopher. Nasir-i Khusrau, the noted traveller and Isma'ili propagandist, was also an eminent figure of that time, but he was not in favour at the court because of his Isma'ili views.

Not long after the death of Malik-Shah, the decline of the Seljuq Empire began. In the north-east the Khwarazmshahs became independent in Transoxiana and ultimately extended their sway over most of Persia. In Fars the Salghurid Atabegs acquired such power as to become independent rulers.

While Muhammad Shah, the ruler of Khwarazm, was extending his power over Persia, far away, beyond the Oxus, the Mongol chieftain Genghis Khan was gathering together his doughty warriors. Mounted on their small but wiry horses, the Mongols swiftly took Samarqand, Bukhara, Balkh and Merv. Though the forces under Muhammad Shah fought bravely, they were overrun and the few surviving remnants were swept aside. After the destruction of Tus and Nishapur, it was the turn of cities farthest west, such as Ray, Qazvin, Kashan and Hamadan. Only the south of Iran escaped the holocaust by swift submission and substantial payments. The loss in human lives and in material things was almost incalculable.

After the Mongol wave had passed on westwards, Jalal al-Din, Muhammad Shah's son, attempted to reorganize the surviving forces, but when the Mongols returned they defeated him. Only isolated pockets of resistance, such as the rulers of the south and the Assassins in certain of their castles, remained unsubdued.

Never, it would seem, was Persian nationhood in greater danger of complete destruction than at the time of the Mongol invasions. Upon the peoples of Islam the assault of this unknown pagan people, seemingly from another world, had the paralysing effect of some great natural disaster. The famous Arab historian Ibn al-Athir remarks in his annalistic history that for some years he was averse from mentioning this event, deeming it so horrible that he shrank from discussing it. It was, he protested, 'the greatest catastrophe and most dire calamity' that had ever overtaken mankind. He refers in particular to the great massacres in the cities of north-eastern Persia, in which astronomical numbers of people were slaughtered. But though the initial impact of these conquests was no less than that produced by the earlier invasions of Alexander and the Arabs, yet their ultimate effect was infinitely less disruptive and may even be said to have paved the way towards the evolution of a national state. Hülegü, the conqueror of Baghdad and the founder of the Il-Khanid state, can be compared, *mutatis mutandis*, with William of Normandy; and if the comparison of a king of England with a Mongol khan appears inept, it is perhaps sufficient to refer to the vengeance exacted by William upon the North of England in 1068, when he 'ravaged the whole country as far as the Tees with fire and sword' and when 'harvest, cattle, the very instruments of husbandry were so mercilessly destroyed that the famine which followed is said to have swept off more than a hundred thousand victims, and half a century later the land still lay bare of culture and deserted of men for sixty miles northward of York'. Whatever the Persians thought of Hülegü, the founder of the dynasty, who, for all his accomplishments as a ruler and a soldier, had the blood of the Caliph on his hands, they cannot but have admired his descendant Ghazan, who, a convert to Islam, had introduced fiscal reforms to alleviate the lot of the peasantry, had charged his vizier Rashid al-Din with composing in Persian the first world history in the full sense ever written and had led his troops to great victories over the Mameluke rulers of Egypt. The struggle with the Mamelukes for the possession of Syria had begun in the time of Hülegü; the last campaign was launched by Ghazan's brother Öljeitü in 1312–13. Throughout this period the Mongol rulers of Persia had sought in vain an alliance with the princes of Europe against their common foe. Ghazan's grandfather Abaqa had been in correspondence with the Pope and Edward I of England; his father Arghun had addressed himself also to Philippe le Bel of France; Ghazan himself in a letter to Pope Boniface VIII apparently refers to a detailed plan for the invasion of Syria which he had previously proposed to the princes of Europe. The significance of this correspondence has not yet been properly evaluated. It was now for the first time since late Antiquity that a centralized state occupying approximately the same area as the Sasanian Empire entered into direct relations with the Christian West. The Il-Khans might, if they had survived longer, have become a truly national dynasty as the Normans, or rather the Angevins did; but the line came to an abrupt end, not because of any inherent weakness, but simply from a shortage of heirs.

Persia was thereupon divided into five separate states, the Chobanids in Azerbaijan, the Jalayirids in western Persia and Baghdad, the Muzaffarids in Fars, the Sarbardarids in Khurasan and the Karts in Herat. The history of these various dynasties is very complicated and the boundaries dividing their realms were frequently changed. Nevertheless, it was an era during which literature flourished to a remarkable extent. The chief star in the poetic firmament was Hafiz.[1]

With the country so divided into small and often antagonistic states, it was no difficult matter for Timur-i Lang ('Lame Timur' or Tamerlane) to invade and conquer it. Just as the Seljuqs had done three centuries earlier, Timur made Persia the central portion of his vast realm. In this new empire Persian culture played a notable part.

In 1402 Timur, in a fiercely contested battle near Ankara, inflicted a shattering defeat on the Ottoman Turks, thus giving the moribund Byzantine Empire another half century of uneasy existence. This victory made a great impression in Europe; one of its consequences was the despatch of the Spanish diplomatic mission under Ruy Gonzales de Clavijo to Timur's court at Samarqand in 1404.

When Timur died in 1405 western Persia was governed by his mentally unstable son Miran Shah and the latter's two sons, while eastern Persia came under the far more capable Shah Rukh, another of the conqueror's offspring. Shah Rukh's wife Gauhar Shad built the beautiful mosque in Mashhad which bears her name.[2]

Timurid control over north-western Persia did not last long, as Miran Shah and his two sons exhausted their strength in fighting one another and so made it easy for Qara Yusuf, the chief of the Turcoman tribe of the Qara Qoyunlu ('Black Sheep') to seize Azerbaijan. Qara Yusuf also drove the Jalayirids from Mesopotamia. Subsequently, Qara Yusuf's son Jahanshah captured Isfahan and the surrounding

[1] See Chapter 3.
[2] See Chapter 5 for details.

territory; after his father's death Jahanshah ruled over all western Persia. Only in eastern Persia did Timurid rule continue under the cultured and talented Shah Rukh, whose seat of government was at Herat. Under his wise and beneficent rule, and that of his son and successor Ulugh Beg, eastern Persia prospered greatly, and poets, artists, musicians, architects and scholars all flourished. Baisunghur, another of Shah Rukh's sons, was a great patron of the arts and was himself an artist and calligrapher of note.[1]

In 1468 the Timurid Sultan Husain ibn Mansur ibn Baiqara made himself ruler of Herat, where he reigned for thirty-eight years. He was a great patron of the arts and was a talented writer himself, as was also his famous minister Mir 'Ali Shir Nava'i.

Previously, in 1467, Jahanshah was defeated and slain by Uzun Hasan ('Long Hasan', who was so called by reason of his height), the chief of the rival Turcoman tribe of the Aq-Qoyunlu ('White Sheep').

Uzun Hasan was a strong and forceful ruler. He allied himself with Kaolo Joannis, the penultimate Emperor of Trebizond, whose daughter Despina Khatun he married. In due course their daughter Maria married Shaikh Haidar of Ardabil; one of their three sons was Isma'il, who was destined to be the founder of the Safavid dynasty. Uzun Hasan was a determined foe of the Ottoman Turks (it must be remembered that they had taken Constantinople in 1453 and were soon threatening the Venetian possessions in the east). The Venetians sought his aid against the Turks on several occasions; the most notable of their envoys to Uzun Hasan were Caterino Zeno, Josafat Barbaro and Ambrogio Contarini. Caterino Zeno managed to induce Uzun Hasan to attack the Ottoman Turks, but they proved too strong for him. Unfortunately, because of the usual reason, namely, bad communications, the Venetians could make no synchronized attack on the Turks.

When Uzun Hasan died in 1478, his sons dissipated much of their strength in the struggle for the succession. After much fighting, Ya'qub, the seventh son, gained the mastery and ruled until 1490. In 1488 Ya'qub had fought a battle with Shaikh Haidar of Ardabil, in the course of which the latter was killed; at that time Haidar's son Isma'il was only one year old. Shaikh Haidar was descended from Shaikh Safi who, at the beginning of the 14th century founded an order of dervishes at Ardabil and established a miniature theocracy there. Shaikh Haidar traced

[1] See Chapter 4.

37

his descent from the Prophet Muhammad through 'Ali's wife Fatima and Musa al-Kazim, the seventh of the Shi'i Imams. He could thus also claim descent from the Sasanian royal line because of the marriage of 'Ali's son Husain to the princess Shahribanu, the daughter of Yazdgird III, the last Sasanian king. It was Shaikh Haidar who gave his followers the famous scarlet cap with twelve gores (one for each of the twelve Imams), which earned for them the name of Qizil-Bash ('Red Heads').

Haidar's son Isma'il spent his early years in hiding from Turcoman and other enemies through the protection of his father's devoted followers, the Sufis of Ardabil. Gradually Isma'il attracted to his banner a number of Shi'i Turcoman tribes from Asia Minor and Syria. Thus he was able eventually to triumph over his enemies. He was crowned Shah of Azarbaijan at Tabriz in 1501. Though as yet in control of a small part of Persia, Isma'il determined that the Ithna 'Ashari branch of the Shi'a (*ie* those recognizing the twelve Imams) should be the accepted and dominant Muslim sect in Persia, though the adherents of the Sunni sect were at that time more numerous in such places as Tabriz.

As the rival Ottoman Turks were staunch Sunnis and began actively to persecute the Shi'is in their realm, Isma'il was able to get widespread support for the Shi'i cause in Persia, and, in due course, a large majority of the inhabitants adopted Shi'ism and accepted Isma'il as their sovereign. Religion constituted one of the strongest unifying forces in the early Safavid era. The Ottoman threat was another factor in Isma'il's success, for, in drawing Iranians together under the Shi'i banner against the encroachments of the Sunni Turks, he reintroduced an element in the Persian social conception that had long been in abeyance. Persia emerged as a nation once again.

Shah Isma'il's success and his enthusiastic championship of Shi'ism aroused the antagonism of Shaibani Khan, the Özbeg leader and exponent of Sunni power in central Asia, and the still more formidable Sultan Selim, the Ottoman Turkish ruler. Shaibani Khan had, in 1507, overcome Sultan Husain, the last Timurid ruler, and he later invaded the province of Kirman. Shah Isma'il responded to this challenge and defeated Shaibani's Özbegs near Merv in 1510; Shaibani himself was among the slain.

Shah Isma'il still, however, had to face his most formidable adversary, Sultan

Selim, who viewed with great disfavour his zeal in the promotion of Shi'ism and his growing military might. The trial of strength came at Chaldiran, in north-west Persia in 1514. The battle was very fiercely contested, but the Turks eventually gained the upper hand largely because they had artillery, while the Persians had none. Moreover, the Turks had their well-trained regular troops, the Janissaries, whereas Shah Isma'il had only tribal levies, whose devotion to their leader, though very marked, proved less effective because of their lack of military training.

Shah Isma'il corresponded with certain Western rulers, particularly the Emperor Charles V, with the object of forming an alliance against the Turks. However, owing to the bad communications between Persia and the West, with a hostile Turkey in between, nothing came of these endeavours. Moreover, Shah Isma'il's contacts with the West were not always friendly, because, owing to his lack of sea power, he had to acquiesce in the Portuguese seizure of the island of Hormuz in 1514, then seen as the key to the Persian Gulf; it was also a place of great commercial importance.

Isma'il was succeeded by his son Tahmasp in 1524. He was a less forceful figure than his father. Neverthless, though he lost part of Kurdistan and Mesopotamia to the Ottoman Turks, he kept intact the main part of Persia. In the earlier part of his reign he was a patron of the arts and was himself an artist and calligrapher. He also did much to encourage the carpet-weaving industry. As a safety measure, he made Qazvin his capital in place of Tabriz, which was far more exposed to Ottoman attack. It was during Tahmasp's long reign that the Russia Company, through the efforts of Anthony Jenkinson, made its gallant effort to open up trade between England and Persia across Russia.

When Tahmasp died in 1576 the throne was briefly occupied by Isma'il II, who was a drunkard and a libertine. His reign, fortunately for Iran and its people, was cut short in 1577 either from poison or an overdose of opium. He was succeeded by his feeble and purblind brother Muhammad Khudabanda. In his incapable hands the Turcoman tribal leaders gained an undue measure of control, and the Turks and Özbegs took advantage of the situation to occupy, respectively, much of north-western and north-eastern Persia.

Fortunately for Persia, at what seemed her blackest hour, the situation was saved by Muhammad Khudabanda's young son 'Abbas whom his supporters placed on the throne after deposing his father in 1587. In the capable hands of the young Shah the tribal leaders were reduced to order and, in due course both the Özbegs and the Ottoman Turks were driven out of the territories that they had occupied. Under the young Shah, the most brilliant period of the Safavid era opened. In 1598 he moved his court from Qazvin to Isfahan and then made the latter city a capital worthy of revitalized Iran. He and his nobles adorned Isfahan with many splendid buildings, making it one of the largest and finest cities of the world.

Shah 'Abbas broke the Turcoman leaders' monopoly of military power by creating a new army paid by himself and manned to a large extent by the sturdy Persian peasants who have always formed such excellent fighting material. He also created an artillery corps. This new fighting force gave an excellent account of itself in the war against the Ottoman Turks. The Western powers, hard pressed by these formidable foes, several times tried to form an alliance with Persia against them, but nothing came of these endeavours. On the other hand, the existence of a powerful military power in their rear lessened the Turks' impact on Europe.

Shah 'Abbas welcomed Europeans to his court, and it is from the vivid accounts of such people as Pietro della Valle and Thomas Herbert that the European world began to realize how resplendent an era it was. The Shah gave the English East India Company trading privileges in Persia and allowed it to set up its factories in Isfahan and elsewhere, but he compelled it, on pain of forfeiture of these privileges, to loan its vessels for use in the successful assault on the Portuguese stronghold of Hormuz in 1622.

One other change made by Shah 'Abbas remains to be mentioned. This was his change of the system of government from a theocracy to one of absolute government.

With the death of Shah 'Abbas and the accession of his grandson Shah Safi in January 1629, the decline of both the dynasty and the country set in. The new Shah neglected the army on which Shah 'Abbas had lavished such care, and he soon showed complete indifference to affairs of state. When under the influence of drink, he had many eminent persons put to death, including a number of military leaders. The consequence was that when the war with the Turks was renewed it was disastrous for Persia, and the Turks were able to regain Baghdad.

When Shah Safi died of the effects of either drink or poison in 1642, his young son 'Abbas mounted the throne. When he reached maturity, he restored the army to its former efficiency and recovered Qandahar from the Mughals (they had captured it in 1637). Unfortunately for Persia, Shah 'Abbas II died at the early age of thirty-three owing to his intemperate ways. Had he lived longer, he might have arrested the decline of the dynasty and of Persia's power.

Shah 'Abbas II was succeeded by his son Shah Sulaiman. Having been brought up in the harem, he was ignorant of affairs of state. He soon fell a victim to the chronic failing of the later Safavids, namely, intemperance. As he became more and more under the influence of drink, he allowed the control of governmental affairs to fall into the hands of the palace eunuchs. The result, as in later Achaemenian times, was an acceleration of the rate of decline. It was fortunate for Persia that the Turks were too engrossed with their wars in Europe to renew their onslaughts on her.

Shah Sulaiman, worn out by his debaucheries, died unlamented in 1694. His successor was the mild and inoffensive Shah Sultan Husain. Like his father, he had been brought up in the harem and so knew nothing of state affairs. Urged on by the Shi'i *ulama*, he allowed them to persecute the formidable Sunni tribe of Lezgis in Daghistan, with the result that a serious revolt broke out. Far worse was to come, however, for in 1722 the Afghan tribe of the Ghilzais, who were also staunch Sunnis, invaded Persia from the east. Though greatly outnumbered, they defeated the royal forces near Isfahan and then marched on and besieged the capital. While the siege was in progress, Tahmasp Mirza, the third son of the Shah, escaped from the city in order to raise a relieving force. This should not have been difficult to do, as there were many loyal elements in various parts of the country; all that they wanted was leadership. Unfortunately, they got none from the young prince, who turned out to be weak and pleasure-loving. He did nothing to relieve the pressure on the beleaguered city, which fell in October 1722, after being besieged for six months. Hundreds of thousands of the inhabitants perished, far more from famine and pestilence than from the Afghan attacks.

Mahmud, the uncouth and brutal Ghilzai leader, thereupon deposed the Shah and mounted the throne himself.

Meanwhile, Persia had received another blow, as Peter the Great invaded northern Persia in the summer of 1722. He did not, however, penetrate further south than Darband, as the Turks threatened him with war if he persisted. The Turks' action was taken not because of any feeling for Persia, but because they had designs on that unfortunate country themselves. In fact, war between Turkey and Russia was averted only by the skilful diplomacy of the Marquis de Bonnac, the French Ambassador to the Porte who induced the two powers to sign a partition treaty respecting Persia. Turkey, in virtue of this treaty, seized much of western and north-western Persia, while the Russians maintained their hold over the north.

Meanwhile Mahmud was maintaining himself in Isfahan, but as time went on he showed signs of madness. One day he broke into the building where the ex-Shah and a number of the young Safavid princes were imprisoned and with his own sword killed many of them. The ex-Shah himself was wounded when trying to protect one of the younger princes. After this terrible deed, Mahmud became completely mad and was himself murdered soon afterwards by adherents of his cousin Ashraf, who then mounted the throne. In the same year (1725) Peter the Great died, and pressure from Russia was somewhat lessened. Meanwhile, however, the Turks had conquered much of western and north-western Persia.

Tahmasp, after wandering in Mazandaran with a handful of men, sought refuge with Fath 'Ali Khan Qajar in the latter's tribal area of Astarabad. While there, Tahmasp received a welcome addition of strength when joined by an adventurer named Nadr Quli Beg at the head of 2,000 of his well-trained Afshar tribesmen. Intense rivalry developed between Fath 'Ali Khan and Nadr Quli Beg which was ended only when Tahmasp, on finding that the Qajar chief was plotting against him, had him executed. Nadr Quli Beg soon gained complete control over the weak prince. Nadr Quli Beg, who was a born soldier, after gaining more adherents, carefully trained his forces; when he deemed that they were ready for battle against the still formidable Ghilzais, he led his men to the attack. In two great battles, first near Damghan and later north of Isfahan, he routed Ashraf and his men. Isfahan was then regained and the Afghans completely defeated. Ashraf himself was murdered in eastern Persia when trying to escape from his pursuers.

Meanwhile, Tahmasp had mounted the vacant throne. Nadr Quli Beg then attacked and drove out the Turks from the areas that they had occupied. A revolt in Khurasan then claimed Nadr's attention. In his absence, Tahmasp foolishly attacked the Turks and was heavily defeated, losing all the territory that Nadr had regained. When Nadr returned from Khurasan, he deposed Tahmasp and placed the latter's infant son 'Abbas on the throne.

In 1733 Nadr attacked the Turks; after an initial defeat, he captured Baghdad. In the following year, he forced Russia to relinquish the territory which she had seized. Subsequently, he renewed the struggle with Turkey and gained a great victory, recapturing Erivan and taking Erzurum.

In the spring of 1736 Nadr, at a great assembly of the nation, formally deposed 'Abbas III and mounted the throne himself, taking the title of Nadir Shah. Later followed Nadir's capture of Qandahar and his subsequent march into India. After heavily defeating the Mughal forces, he marched south and occupied Delhi, where he obtained immense spoils.

On his way back to Persia, Nadir advanced northwards and subdued the Özbegs of Bukhara and Khiva. When he reached Persia he suspected his eldest son Riza Quli Mirza of wishing to retain the powers which he had entrusted to him before the Indian expedition. In consequence, he had the unfortunate prince blinded, an action which he ever afterwards regretted. From that time, fate, which had hitherto seemed to favour him, failed to do so – though he did gain another victory over the Turks. The terrible exactions of his tax collectors and his executions of many of his ministers and officials led to his murder in Khurasan in 1747. As a military leader he could rank with Timur, but when it came to governing the country and preparing the ground for his successors, he was a signal failure.

Nadir's death was followed by the usual scramble for the throne, from which, after a period of confusion, Karim Khan Zand, of Luristan, emerged as the victor. He turned out to be one of the best and mildest rulers that Persia has ever had. Shiraz was his capital city. He never claimed the title of Shah, being content with that of *Vakil* or 'Deputy'. As was so often the case, his heirs and successors squandered their energies and lives in struggles for the throne, with the result that they exhausted themselves and so opened the way for the accession of Agha Muhammad Khan Qajar, the grandson of the man whom Tahmasp had executed for treason. The new ruler of Persia had, when very young, fallen into the hands of 'Adil Shah, Nadir Shah's brutal nephew, who made his unfortunate captive a eunuch, an act which permanently embittered him. Agha Muhammad was cold, calculating and intensely cruel. Sir John Malcolm said of him:[1] 'The first

---

[1] *History of Persia*, London, 1815, Vol 11, p 306.

passion of his mind was the love of power, the second, avarice, and the third, revenge.'

After uniting the various branches of the Qajar tribe, he captured Tehran and made it his capital. He then, by degrees, made himself master of the whole of Persia, but it was not until 1795 that he took the title of Shah. Two years later he was assassinated. His stern rule, though marred by frequent acts of cruelty, gave the country some much-needed tranquillity. Furthermore, by his strengthening of the Qajar tribe, he made more secure the position of his nephew and successor Fath'Ali Shah.

The new monarch, who reigned from 1797 to 1834, was unwise enough to wage war twice on Russia, and lost much territory in consequence. These defeats were caused by his army's lack of training and of modern weapons. Fath 'Ali Shah was himself largely responsible for these defeats, as he was too parsimonious to provide the necessary funds to provide the proper equipment for his troops.

It was during Fath 'Ali Shah's reign that British influence first became noticeable in Persia, first against France and later against Russia.

When Fath 'Ali Shah died in 1834, he was succeeded by his son Muhammad. The new monarch's predominant desire was to make up for his country's territorial losses to Russia by taking territory in the east at the expense of the Afghans. In this aim he was strongly supported by Russia. Great Britain, however, fearing that such expansion towards India might enable Russia to increase her threat to that country, sought to dissuade the Shah, but failed to do so. Muhammad Shah then marched on Herat and besieged it. However, the defenders, helped and inspired by a British artillery officer called Pottinger, successfully held out. Great Britain forced Muhammad Shah to withdraw by seizing the island of Kharg in the Persian Gulf.

Meanwhile, Great Britain and Russia, for once acting in agreement, persuaded Persia and Turkey to appoint a frontier commission to delimit their common frontier, a task which was completed by the signature of the Treaty of Erzurum in 1847.

The new Shah was only seventeen when he mounted the throne. In the early years of his reign, Nasir al-Din's incorruptible and very able Vizier Mirza Taqi Khan, the Amir-i Nizam, took some steps to modernize the country. Education was stimulated, a newspaper was started and other reforms were attempted. Taqi

Khan's reforming achievements made him many enemies and ultimately caused his downfall and murder.

Later in the reign postal services between various towns were introduced, as was also the telegraph system. Security in the country was rigidly enforced.

During the second half of Nasir al-Din's reign many foreigners visited Persia, while the Shah himself went to Europe three times.

The last few years of the reign were disturbed by the strong opposition to the tobacco concession, which the Shah had granted to a British company, and also by the growing demands for reform. On the 6th May 1896, the Shah was murdered by a fanatic. Though he had obvious faults, he had many compensating qualities and can be regarded as far the best of the Qajar monarchs.

Nasir al-Din's son and successor, Muzaffar al-Din, though kindly by nature, was lacking in initiative and fixity of purpose. He had neither the will nor the ability to deal successfully with the rapidly mounting political feeling. Yielding at last to popular pressure, he dismissed his unpopular Vizier, the 'Ain al-Dauleh, and later signed a *farman* (royal rescript) for the convening of a National Assembly which was to draw up and pass an electoral law. This body duly met, drafted the law and passed it, with the result that the elections were held and the first Majlis (National Assembly) met in October 1906. In the following December it passed the Fundamental Law of the Constitution which was signed by the Shah on the 30th December, five days before his death. This Fundamental Law provided Persia with a constitution resembling, in a number of respects, the Belgian constitution.

Practically all classes of the people, including the *'ulama*, had participated in the struggle for the Constitution.

Muhammad 'Ali Shah, the new monarch, though he swore to respect the constitution, showed nothing but contempt for the Majlis. Soon after his accession the people of Tabriz intercepted a large consignment of arms which the Shah had ordered from Russia; previously, his agents had attempted to suppress the constitutionalists in that city.

The Anglo-Russian Agreement, which was concluded in 1907, caused consternation in Iran. This agreement, whereby that country was divided into three zones, one where Russian influence was predominant, one where that of Great Britain was to prevail, and one neutral, was negotiated without any consultation with, or previous notice to the Iranian Government. The manner in which it was concluded was in itself an affront to Iran which not all the fine phrases about preserving her sovereignty and keeping her territory intact could palliate.

In May 1907 the Majlis had approved the Supplementary Fundamental Law whereby certain gaps in the original Law were filled. It was only with extreme difficulty that the Shah was induced to approve this Law. He soon showed that he had no intention of being bound by it. In the summer of 1908 he took the extreme measure of declaring martial law and then directing his troops, who were under the command of a Russian officer, to bombard the Majlis, killing and wounding a number of deputies. The Shah thereupon resorted to absolute rule. In Tabriz, where a revolt broke out, he was able to suppress it only with the aid of Russian troops.

The Shah's high-handed measures and his open contempt for the Constitution led to the formation of a strong nationalist movement the forces of which routed those of the Shah whom they then formally deposed, placing his eldest son Ahmad, then aged eleven, on the throne. The ex-Shah fled to Russia. In the following year he took advantage of a split among the constitutionalists to return to Persia, but he was soon defeated and forced to return to Russia.

The national finances were by this time in chaos, and an attempt to put them in order was made by an American named Morgan Shuster and a number of assistants. This development was eventually rendered nugatory by Russia's opposition. Great Britain could not interfere because of her signature to the Anglo-Russian Agreement, and Shuster and his assistants had to leave the country.

Subsequently, the Russians seized Tabriz where they behaved with great brutality; their behaviour in Mashhad was even worse, as they bombarded and damaged the shrine of the Imam Riza.

In June 1914 the young Shah Ahmad was crowned. Only a few weeks later the First World War broke out. Persia declared her neutrality, but her sympathies lay with Germany, since she regarded any foe of Russia as a friend. The entry of Turkey into the war as an ally of Germany and her violation of Persian territory in order to attack Russia, led that power also to violate Persian soil. Moreover, fear of a Turkish attempt in the south to destroy the refinery of the Anglo-Persian Oil Company at Abadan and the pipe-line from the oilfields, led to British intervention in that area. Another reason for the presence of British troops in the south was that Germany and Turkey both planned to send troops across Persia to Afghanistan.

As was natural, these moves and counter-moves by the rival powers were most trying to the Persians. When Russia collapsed in 1917, Great Britain was left in a position of great influence in Persia. After the war was over, Great Britain endeavoured to negotiate an agreement with Persia which, while guaranteeing her independence, would nevertheless give Great Britain much influence there.

The negotiations for this agreement aroused much opposition in Persia, and its ratification by the Majlis was eventually rejected.

Events soon took a dramatic turn. In February 1921 Sayyid Ziya al-Din Tabataba'i, a young politician with liberal views, and Riza Khan, the able commander of the Cossack Brigade, marched on the capital. The Government fell and Sayyid Ziya became Prime Minister while Riza Khan was made Commander-in-Chief. Riza Khan's outstanding ability as a soldier had already been noted by knowledgeable men both inside and outside Persia.

Three months after the *coup d'état*, Riza Khan and Sayyid Ziya quarrelled, with the result that the latter had to resign and leave the country. Sayyid Ziya had, apparently, been too precipitate and drastic in some of his actions. Under his successor Riza Khan became Minister of War, and in 1923 he was himself appointed Prime Minister.

Riza Khan was firmly of the opinion that a strong army was essential for the carrying out of his policy of restoring the authority of the Government throughout the country. He fused together the Cossack Brigade, the South Persia Rifles and the gendarmerie. With this force he reduced the dissident tribes to order.

In 1922 Turkey, under the leadership of Kemal Ataturk, abolished the Caliphate and established a republic, with Ataturk as President. In the following year there was a movement in Persia to set up a republic and make Riza Khan President. However, the Turks' abolition of the Caliphate and certain other anti-Islamic acts aroused unfavourable feelings in Persia with the result that the idea of a republic there was dropped.

The ineffectual Ahmad Shah left Persia on a visit to Europe in 1923. As he was still absent in 1925 the Majlis formally declared that the Qajar dynasty was terminated and called for the convening of a Constituent Assembly for the purpose of making the necessary changes to the constitutional laws. In the meantime, the provisional government of the country was entrusted to Riza Khan. On the 12th December 1925 the Constituent Assembly, by an overwhelming majority, declared that the constitutional sovereignty of Persia was to be entrusted by the people to 'His Imperial Majesty Riza Shah Pahlavi' and that it was to pass 'to his male descendants, generation by generation'. In April 1926 the coronation ceremony took place. A new chapter in Persian history had begun.

ABOVE
Shapur the Great receiving the homage of the
Roman Emperor Valerian
Collection of L. P. Elwell-Sutton

BELOW
The Mausoleum of the Seljuq Sultan Sanjar at
Merv
Collection of L. P. Elwell-Sutton

2

The Pahlavi Era

L. P. ELWELL-SUTTON

The accession of HIM Riza Shah Pahlavi to the throne on 15th December 1925, marked the inauguration of the Pahlavi Dynasty. But it did not mark the beginning of the Pahlavi era, which may be said to have begun with the march on Tehran and the *coup d'état* of 21st February 1921. Although Riza Khan, largely responsible for the success of that stroke of state, did not reward himself with the highest office and was content to serve as Commander-in-Chief of the Armed Forces, it was only a matter of months before his dominating personality began to make its mark. The coronation ceremony five years later was the culminating recognition of the individual impression that he had stamped on the affairs of his country. He became Minister of War in April 1921, and Prime Minister in October 1923; but most of these early years of office were taken up with the basic task of restoring order throughout the country and establishing the authority of the Central Government. In a systematic series of campaigns round the country he suppressed three politically inspired rebellions in the north of Iran, and a number of tribal risings in the south and west. However his greatest triumph, and one that undoubtedly paved the way

ABOVE
The Amir Kabir Dam at Karaj, near Tehran
Collection of L. P. Elwell-Sutton

BELOW
The Shahyad Monument at Tehran, commemorating the 2500th anniversary of the foundation of the Persian Monarchy
Collection of L. P. Elwell-Sutton

for his final elevation to supreme power, was his taming of the recalcitrant Shaikh of Muhammereh.[1] Though in the end the Shaikh's resistance collapsed without a blow in face of the inexorable advance of the new powerful Chief Minister from Tehran, the decision to take this action required a good deal of courage and resolution. The Shaikh believed himself to be in an impregnable position. He had, he thought, the support of a wide range of tribal chieftains in the southern provinces; his domains included the oilfields and installations of the Anglo-Persian Oil Company, in which the British Government held a majority share; and he had been given reason to think that the British Government (which did indeed send warships to the Persian Gulf) would support him in his clash with the Central Government in Tehran. In the end none of these expectations materialized. The local population remained apathetic, tribal unrest faded away and even the British, after their initial sabre-rattling, recognized that the pacification and reunification of the country was no bad thing. Riza Khan arrived in Muhammereh on 28th November 1924, accepted the surrender of the Shaikh (who was subsequently removed to exile in Tehran), and a month later returned to the capital to be greeted with a triumphal reception.

The first action of the Iranian Parliament (the Majlis) was to invest Riza Khan with full powers; but everyone realized that this could only lead to one final result. In November 1923, the young and ineffectual Ahmad Shah Qajar had left for Europe, never to return. Early in 1924 there had been much talk of the establishment of a republic, with Riza Khan as the first president; but this scheme had foundered on the opposition of the religious authorities, worried by Mustafa Kemal Pasha's recent abolition of the Ottoman Caliphate in Turkey, as well as on the instinctive liking of the Iranians for the monarchical form of government. By the autumn of 1925 the logic of events had become irresistible; on 31st October the Majlis deposed the Qajar dynasty, appointed Riza Khan as Head of State, and set up a Constituent Assembly, which on 12th December amended the Constitution so as to invest the monarchy in the person of Riza Shah Pahlavi and his successors in the male line.

Though throughout his reign Riza Shah maintained and respected the forms of democracy in the shape of the Constitution, by holding regular elections and ensuring that the Majlis duly met and debated and ratified the legislation initiated

---

[1] The modern Khurramshahr.

by his cabinets under his guidance, yet there can be no doubt that the period between 1925 and 1941 was the era of Riza Shah. This was not just a question of the ubiquitous portraits that symbolized his omnipresence; virtually every step that was taken, every reform that was introduced, was typical of his ruthless innovation. For anxious as he was that Iranians should participate fully in the government of their country, he was equally aware that the century and a half of stagnation and apathy that had preceded his reign could only be overcome by the forceful methods characteristic of an authoritarian rather than a popular democratic regime. There was still much to be done. By 1925 a fair degree of security and stability had been established throughout the country, but in almost every other respect Iran was still a semi-medieval society. Communications were almost non-existent; even the main highways were little more than rough tracks, scarcely passable by the horse-drawn carriages that were almost the only wheeled transport available. There were no significant railways; the telegraph system was limited to what had been constructed by the British-established Indo-European Telegraph Company during the 19th century as a link in the international network connecting Europe with India. Industry (apart from the British-owned and operated oil industry) was still in the handicraft stage. A number of private and public schools had been established during the preceding twenty-five years (in addition to a handful of foreign mission schools), but modern education was still the privilege of a small minority. The majority of the population, even in the towns, was illiterate. The picture as regards health services, doctors, hospitals and dispensaries was not very different. And above all, particularly in those sections of the community who ought to have been giving a lead to the country, there was a lack of direction and an absence of patriotic sentiment and community feeling.

All this had to be changed, and if it seemed that in the early stages there was excessive concentration on strengthening the power of the Central Government, this was only because Riza Shah's experience had taught him that the kind of revolution that he was planning, a revolution that was to change drastically and for the better the way of life of great sections of the population, could only be pushed through under strong centralized direction. So first of all an army had to be created – for the miscellaneous forces that Riza Khan had inherited as Commander-in-Chief in 1921 could hardly be dignified by that description. Established initially at 40,000, it had by 1941 been steadily built up to a figure of 200,000, still a comparatively small force designed to maintain internal security rather than to repel invasion from outside. To this land force was added in due course a small navy with vessels on the Caspian Sea and the Persian Gulf, and the nucleus of an air force. As tribal unrest subsided, security outside the towns was entrusted to a body of road guards organized as a subsidiary branch of the army, while a properly organized police force was established in the urban areas. Within the machinery of government itself, the haphazard methods of the past were replaced by an orderly bureaucratic structure, a bureaucracy indeed that, in the view of some, became over-rigid and centralized as time went on, but without which it is doubtful whether much progress could have been made in other fields. The confused medley of Islamic and customary law was replaced by civil and criminal codes based on European models, and the administration of justice was taken out of the hands of the religious authorities and entrusted to a professional corps of lawyers under the supervision of the Ministry of Justice. This permitted in 1928 the abolition of the Capitulations, the system established early in the 19th century by which foreign nationals had the right to be tried in their own consular courts instead of submitting to Iranian justice. The financial structure of the country was reorganized, taxation and government budgeting placed on a systematic basis, the note issue transferred from the British-owned Imperial Bank of Iran to the newly formed National Bank (Bank Milli), and other banks and insurance companies established under state control.

All this took time, and meanwhile it was essential to open up communications throughout the country if these schemes for centralized government were to become effective. So an ambitious programme of road construction was inaugurated, which by 1940 had resulted in the completion of over 15,000 miles of roads which, though unsurfaced and still well below the standards usual in Western Europe or the United States, were at least negotiable in all weathers, particularly by the heavy lorries that for most of the country were long to remain the only means of transporting goods from the rural to the urban areas and *vice-versa*. Meanwhile in August 1938, after eleven years of often frustrated effort, the Shah personally tightened the last golden bolt in the massive achievement of the Transiranian Railway, cutting across the country from the Caspian port of Bandar Shah in the north to the Persian Gulf harbour of Bandar Shahpur in the south. Though in Riza Shah's lifetime no further railway construction was to take place, the new line was to become the nucleus of a network covering the whole country, and meanwhile it stood as the most impressive symbol of what could be achieved by a small 'backward' country determined to pursue its own policies and to make use of western technological expertise to further its own interests and not those of other nations.

The building of roads and railways was accompanied in a natural sequence by the development of industry. Once again the Shah had to build virtually from scratch, and the major effort was put into the construction of factories that would utilize Iranian products – sugar beet, silk, cotton, tobacco, fruit, fish – as well as light industries like cement, textiles, glass, paper, chemicals, soap and iron founding. Nearly all of these were state owned, and a number of products – sugar, tea, tobacco, for example – were controlled by state monopolies, while the import-export business was subject to protective tariffs and currency restrictions. Only the oil industry, in spite of being Iran's major industry, remained wholly outside the government's net, though as we shall see it was not altogether undisturbed.

The motive behind all this activity was not exclusively commercial. There were two main purposes – to make Iran gradually independent of foreign sources of supply, and to set the country firmly on the path towards a modern, industrialized society. The modernization of Iranian life was indeed one of Riza Shah's dominating ambitions. He wanted his people to think of themselves as in no way inferior to the peoples of the West, and he wanted foreigners to be aware of and respect the good qualities of Iranians. There were two principal ways in which this could be done, in his view – on the one hand borrowing what was useful in Western technology and culture, and on the other hand reviving a uniquely Iranian culture on the basis of what was sound in the tradition of the past. So we find on the one hand drastic programmes of urbanization and town planning, in which broad tree-planted avenues cut ruthlessly across the tangled bazaars of the old oriental towns, and the enclosed courtyards of the traditional Iranian houses gave way to modern blocks of flats. Sport and physical education were encouraged. If people were to work in factories and to engage in football, they could no longer wear the traditional flowing garments of the past, and so these had to be replaced by European dress. The tribes, whose nomadic way of life was both incompatible with a modern society and a constant threat to urban stability and safe travel, had to be settled on the land, no matter how this might disrupt their accustomed life and livelihood. On the other hand the public buildings that were erected in the cities often reflected not the box-like structures of Europe but the ancient architecture of Achaemenid Persepolis and Sasanian Ctesiphon. The glories of Iran's ancient past were resuscitated in other ways – for instance, in the celebration on an international scale in 1934 of the millenary of Iran's great national poet Firdausi. A brief attempt was even made to purge the Persian language of its huge enrichment of Arabic words.

Probably, however, Riza Shah's most spectacular modernizing reform was the abolition of the Islamic veil in 1936, the first step on the long road to the complete emancipation of women. Thereafter women were encouraged to acquire education, to enter the professions, business and industry. Girls had already been drawn into the new state system of schools and colleges, virtually created under the regime of Riza Shah and crowned in 1935 by the foundation of the University of Tehran. The effects of this sudden expansion of educational facilities was to be seen not only in the increasing degree to which Iranians were able to fill posts in commerce and industry that required more than basic skills, but also in the intellectual and literary revival that, in spite of the strict censorship, was a marked feature of these years.

Riza Shah's foreign policy aimed at securing Iran's independence and in particular eliminating the influence of the great powers whose rivalries had for so long plagued the country. He hoped to achieve this by encouraging and participating in international organizations like the League of Nations, by adhering to treaties like the Kellogg Pact for the outlawing of war, and at the same time by co-operating with Iran's immediate neighbours. The crowning achievement of this policy was the signing in Tehran in 1937 of the Saadabad Pact between Iran, Turkey, Iraq and Afghanistan, concurrent with which was the settlement of a variety of frontier and other disputes that had for many years disturbed relations between these states. Riza Shah's only serious clash with a foreign power arose in 1932 over the Anglo-Persian Oil Company's concession in the south. Though once again there was some sabre-rattling by Britain in the Persian Gulf, the dispute was finally resolved through international channels, and the following year a new concession was negotiated that brought considerable benefits to both sides.

Unfortunately this cautious foreign policy was not to stand the Shah in very good stead after World War Two had broken out in 1939. Although Iran declared her strict neutrality from the outset, the sudden reversal of the war situation in June, 1941, by the German invasion of Russia brought the Middle East in general and Iran in particular once again into the centre of world affairs. The Western Allies, desperate to find a means of conveying war supplies to the Soviet Union, could see only one route open to them, the one through Iran. Under the stress of war the usual courtesies were ignored, and after a brief propaganda campaign by Britain and Russia aimed ostensibly against the presence of German technicians working in Iran, on 25th August 1941, the two powers invaded the country from north and south. On 16th September the Shah, recognizing the impossibility of his continuing to reign over an occupied country, abdicated in favour of his son Muhammad Riza and left his homeland never to return. Another watershed in Iran's history had been reached.

For the next dozen years the direction of Iranian political and social life was to be changed. In violent reaction against the authoritarianism of the previous two decades, the progressive and constructive activities of the ex-Shah were abandoned, and instead Iranians poured their energies into politics, something that had been almost forgotten. Political parties sprang up on all sides, notably those formed by left-wing activists newly released from prison. Newspapers, hitherto used primarily as media for the propagation of Riza Shah's reform policies, now became political pamphlets supporting the views of this or that grouping or personality; the views expressed not only the anti-authoritarian attitudes that had now become fashionable, but also the anti-Fascist and anti-Nazi postures dictated by Iran's new association with the Allied Powers. In the north particularly, where Russian influence was dominant, the 'left-wing' point of view found easiest expression; elsewhere there was a more wide-ranging freedom of thought, though the general trend was set by the colour of the frequently changing cabinets. Meanwhile the economic situation of the country, exacerbated by the insatiable demands of the occupying forces as well as by hoarding of grain and profiteering, grew steadily worse. By 1944 the cost of living had risen seven times over its 1941 figure. In December 1942 serious bread riots in Tehran resulted in the wholesale suppression of the press for a period of six weeks, and even the arrival in January 1943 of an American financial mission under the redoubtable Dr Millspaugh, who had previously served in Iran from 1921 to 1927, failed to make much impact on the situation.

After the German defeat at Stalingrad the tide of war began to recede from the Middle East. This meant in practice that Iran, who had signed a tripartite treaty with Britain and Russia in January 1942, was emboldened to join the United Nations and in September 1943 to declare war on Germany. In December the three Allied leaders, Churchill, Stalin and Roosevelt, meeting at the Tehran Conference, issued a declaration confirming Iran's independence and promising economic aid after the end of the war. In the meantime the three powers had taken over the operation of the railway, as well as much of the road transport of the country, though Iran was able to benefit later from the rail and road improvements carried out by the occupying forces.

By contrast the removal of the external military threat contributed to the polarization of Iranian domestic politics. This was also partly a reflection of the 'East-West' polarization in international affairs. The first major political party to have made its appearance was the Tudeh (Masses) Party, which during 1942 had succeeded in gaining the support of a wide spectrum of anti-Fascist and social democratic opinion, but as time went on came to be more and more associated both in the public mind and in practice with the views and interests of the Soviet Union. For some time the 'right-wing' opposition remained without any leader or organization. But in August 1943 Sayyid Ziya al-Din, who had collaborated in 1921 with Riza Khan and became the first Prime Minister after the *coup d'état* of that year, returned from exile and in due course, as the leader of the Iradeh-yi Milli (National Will) Party, gathered around him the growing hostility to the pro-Soviet policies of the left. During 1944 the left-right conflict became overt in the reaction to a Soviet request, brought by a special mission to Tehran headed by Commissar S. I. Kavtaradze, for an oil concession in the north of Iran. The ensuing furore culminated in a decision, put forward in the first place by Dr Muhammad Musaddiq, to defer any consideration of such requests until after the war. But now the knives were, metaphorically, out, and even the end of the European war in May 1945 brought no relief. Now argument centred round the question of when the Allied forces would quit Iran. The Americans left at the end of 1945, the last British troops moved out on 2nd March 1946, while the Russians did not finally evacuate until 9th May. But in the meantime events had taken place that were to prove vital for Iran and significant for the rest of the world.

In September 1945 the left-wing groupings in Azerbaijan, the north-western province of Iran then under Soviet occupation, broke off their somewhat uneasy relationship with the Tudeh Party in Tehran and formed the Democrat Party of Azerbaijan, pledged to greater autonomy for the province. During November they broke into open revolt against the Central Government, and proclaimed an autonomous government with its capital at Tabriz. The Russian authorities refused to allow Iranian troops to enter the province, and the Tehran government, fearful of provoking a clash with Iran's powerful northern neighbour, drew back, and, under British and American encouragement, referred the matter to the Security Council – the first case to be heard by that body. The debates there were protracted and inconclusive, but in the meantime the Iranian premier resigned and was succeeded by Qavam al-Saltaneh, an ageing and wily politician of the old school. In a series of brilliant manoeuvres, Qavam recognised the autonomy of Azerbaijan, promised the Russians an oil concession and secured the withdrawal of their troops, suppressed the right-wing opposition and formed his own middle of the road Democrat Party of Iran, coaxed the left-wing parties into an alliance and took three Tudeh Party ministers into his cabinet. He then suddenly turned on the left, expelled the Tudeh Cabinet Ministers, and exploited a tribal rising in the south to turn public opinion against provincial autonomy. In December the Shah sent Iranian troops on a virtually unopposed expedition into the province of Azerbaijan, where the autonomous government melted away and the authority of the Central Government was re-established. During the following year the Majlis, to Qavam's ill-concealed delight, rejected his proposal to offer the Soviet Union an oil concession, and he resigned office with his task virtually complete.

The defeat of the left had two important consequences for the political scene in Iran, one comparatively short-term, the other with more lasting effects. While prime ministers and governments continued to succeed one another with bewildering frequency and with little positive effect, in the country at large a confederation of nationalist groupings, led by the Musaddiq who had helped to thwart the Soviet demand for an oil concession, formed the Jabheh-yi Milli (National Front) and attracted support from many who had no use for either the left-wing extremists or the fumbling incompetence of the old-style politicians who formed the bulk of the cabinets. At the same time the young Shah, who during the occupation of his country by foreign forces had prudently remained in the background while in no way yielding his sovereign status, began to grow in prestige and authority. An abortive attempt on his life in February 1949 served both to enhance his personal popularity and further to discredit the forces of the left, who were held responsible for the incident. But before he could be restored to the position his father had held as unquestioned ruler of the country, Iran was to pass through yet another traumatic episode.

Though the National Front incorporated within its ranks a great many different political points of view, it was not long before they were able to find common ground in opposition to the British-owned Anglo-Iranian Oil Company, whose monopolistic control of the Iranian oil industry had been only momentarily jolted by the Irano-Soviet oil negotiations. The 1933 concession was now seen to be inadequate and out-of-date, but while succeeding governments concentrated on negotiating better terms, the National Front favoured more extreme measures, and when Musaddiq, riding on a wave of nationalist fervour, became Prime Minister in April 1951, his first action was to cancel the concession and nationalize the oil industry. An increasingly high-powered series of British and Anglo-American negotiating missions foundered on the obstinate insistence of the elderly premier that the operation of the oil industry must be in Iranian hands, and in October the company withdrew from its areas in the south-west to a shrill chorus of delight from Tehran. But Musaddiq had miscalculated, not so much the technical problems of working the oil industry, which were by no means beyond the capacity of Iranians, as the strength of the international oil cartel and the support it had from most of the major world powers. The consequent economic difficulties in which Iran found herself led to growing domestic tension. Musaddiq found himself being pulled more and more towards the left, now experiencing something of a revival; and desperately seeking to counter this tendency by building up his own position, he came into conflict with the Shah who, whatever sympathy he might feel for the general objectives of the nationalist movement, was not prepared to surrender any of his authority to a man and a party whose precipitate approach to problems seemed to stem from weakness rather than from strength. In August 1953 matters came to a head; in a successful *coup d'état* General Zahidi, acting on behalf of the Shah, defeated the largely left-wing opposition, and the Shah returned in triumph to his throne.

From this point the direction of affairs returned once again to the sovereign; but the task that faced the Shah was somewhat different from the one with which his father had had to deal when he took over supreme power twenty-eight years earlier. Certainly there was still a problem of internal security and stability, but now it was not a matter of tribal unrest but of political subversion by remnants of the National Front and the Tudeh Party. The Shah therefore saw as the first necessity the purging of these elements from the armed forces and political life. It was because of the concentration on this policy that the early years after 1953 gave the appearance of years largely devoted to the negative suppression of political activity rather than to constructive reforms. In fact this impression did not depict the whole story. One other major task that faced Iran was the settlement of the oil problem, so that the country could once again enjoy the economic and financial benefits of a thriving industry. In the view of the Shah and his experts the time had not yet come for Iran to exploit her oil resources without external aid, and so negotiations were started with an international consortium representing all of the major and many of the minor oil companies adhering to the international petroleum cartel. Agreement was reached towards the end of 1954, and very soon the oil installations of the south-west were once again operating at full output. Nevertheless the ultimate ownership and control was now vested in the National Iranian Oil Company, so preserving the principle of nationalization, and the tide was running strongly against the granting of semi-monopolies of Iran's resources to foreign organizations. Over the succeeding years a variety of agreements were concluded with both cartel and independent companies in respect of land areas outside the consortium's zone and of offshore areas in the Persian Gulf, under which an increasing share of both financial interest and operational control was retained by the Iranian Government.

The same years also witnessed considerable expansion in the industrial and economic fields. In a number of respects however the changed national and international situation called for a different approach from that adopted by Riza Shah. Although in the broadest sense the direction of Iranian affairs after 1953 could be said to have been a continuation of the 1925–41 policies, that is to say, the establishment of Iranian independence on the basis of political, economic and social stability, certain policies were altered and even reversed. State control of industry was largely abandoned, and encouragement was given to the development of private enterprise. Shares in state-owned factories were sold on the open market, and in some cases government concerns were disposed of altogether. Investment funds were sought from abroad, and some effort was made to preserve a balance between the two sides of the international power bloc situation by seeking interest from Eastern Europe as well as from the United States and Western Europe. In the field of finance the state monopoly was relaxed, and a large number of private banks and insurance companies were formed, some purely Iranian, others with substantial participation by foreign interests.

Agriculture also came in for considerably more attention than in the past. Even before the launching of the land reform (of which more will be said in a moment), a variety of steps had been taken to improve agricultural production by ameliorating the condition of peasants and landworkers, the establishment of experimental farms, the afforestation of desert areas, pest control measures, and the extension of irrigation schemes. A large number of dams were constructed, notably the Amir Kabir Dam on the Karaj River near Tehran, the Shahbanu Farah Dam on the Safidrud River in Gilan, and the Muhammad Riza Shah Dam on the Diz River in Khuzistan. Most of these were designed to provide water for both rural and urban needs. The rural areas also benefited from the expansion and reconstruction of the road, rail and air networks, which brought Iran into the lead in the Middle East in respect of rapid transport.

In general the outlook of Iran became increasingly international. The Shah himself embarked on the series of journeys abroad that marked all the subsequent years of his reign, and showed himself willing and able to meet and talk with foreign journalists as well as officials and politicians. In 1960 his autobiography was published in several European languages. Iran signed the Baghdad Pact in 1955, and when that organization disintegrated after the withdrawal of Iraq in 1958, was instrumental in the creation of CENTO and other regional groupings. While accepting a substantial degree of financial and economic aid from the United States, Iran was anxious not to seem too closely aligned with any one of the international power blocs, and succeeded in maintaining friendly relations and developing economic links with both the Soviet Union and the People's Republic of China. The growing problems of the countries of the Arab world as a result of the Arab-

Israeli conflict and of internal political upheavals enabled the more stable Iran to take an increasingly prominent part in the affairs of the Middle East, and especially in the Persian Gulf, where after the final British withdrawal in the seventies Iran was to become the dominant power. The steady build-up in Iranian armed forces, which might at first sight have seemed excessive in relation to the domestic security situation, could now be seen to have been a preparation for the day when Iran would become a country with international obligations and responsibilities.

By 1957 it seemed that the country was ready for a fresh injection of political responsibility. The negative repression of the post-1953 period was eased off, and two major political parties, the Milliyun (Nationalists) and Mardum (People) Parties, were formed. At the same time a degree of freedom was given to other political groupings, including even some representatives of the defunct National Front. That this was a genuine attempt at introducing more democratic institutions is suggested by the fact that the experiment continued for several years, even though it seemed frequently on the point of breaking down. Eventually however it became clear that the kind of technocratic society towards which Iran was now moving was incompatible with the type of political free-for-all which the party system inevitably seemed to produce in Iran.

At the beginning of 1963 the Shah launched what has come to be known as the White Revolution, or the Revolution of the Shah and the People. The latter title makes it evident that the intention of the sovereign was to bypass the political party establishment and to seek a direct link with the electorate. In fact the first step took precisely this form. This was a referendum on a six-point programme of drastic reform which, since it dealt with some of Iran's most long standing social evils, was assured in advance of the massive support that it received. Over a period of time another thirteen points were added, covering the whole spectrum of Iranian economic and social affairs. They included reform of the landownership system, nationalization of forests, pastures and water resources, co-ownership and profit-sharing in industry, measures against profiteering and corruption, a national insurance scheme, the extension of literacy, health and development to the rural areas, electoral reform (which meant in particular votes for women), local courts in rural areas for the settlement of minor disputes, educational reform and the provision of free education.

Of these the most impressive were the Land Reform and the Literacy, Health and Development Corps. Under the first of these the age-old land tenure system, which permitted the growth of huge estates owned by absentee landlords and left the peasant at the bottom of the pile with little or no hope of improvement of his status, was abolished. A low upper limit was set on individual holdings, and the rest of the land was transferred to the peasants, who operated it through village co-operatives. The introduction of the three corps was a measure designed to make more practical use of the abilities of a proportion of the young men (and later women) called up for national service in the armed forces. National servicemen with educational qualifications were, after a brief period of normal military training, seconded to rural areas to set up small classes for children and adults to give them the rudiments of literacy. Later the two other corps were added to provide a similar service in the fields of health and hygiene, improvement of buildings and sanitation, modern agricultural methods, encouragement of handicrafts, and other such activities.

The extension of the suffrage to women was another important step, still almost unique among Moslem countries. From that time on women, already prominent in many professions, entered both houses of parliament and were appointed to cabinet posts. Women's interests were further advanced by the passing in 1967 of the Family Protection Law, which placed women almost on a par with men in the fields of marriage and divorce, inheritance of property, custody of children, and so on. The great expansion of the university system, from the single Tehran University founded by Riza Shah to the twenty-one universities and various other institutions of higher education in Tehran and the provinces, provided women as well as men with much-enhanced opportunities for advanced training. The progress of women during these years owed much to the interest and encouragement of the Shahbanu (Empress), to whose support also must be attributed the growing attention to cultural matters, particularly the revival of traditional Iranian arts and crafts.

In the summer of 1973 the last page was turned in the long saga of the Iranian oil industry. By means of peaceful negotiation, largely the work of the Shah himself, the result that Musaddiq and the National Front had failed to achieve twenty-two years earlier by aggressive and ill-planned measures was finally realized. By agreement with the Consortium the full control and operation of the industry was trans-

ferred to Iran; after seventy-two years beginning with the D'Arcy Concession of
1901, Iran's oil became once more fully Iranian. One important effect of this agreement was that Iran was enabled to play an even more dominant role in the Organization of Petroleum Exporting Countries (OPEC), particularly in the areas of price-
fixing and control of exploitation. The inflationary situation in the Western World
made this more than ever imperative, since it was only by regular and in some
cases drastic increases in the price of oil that the producing countries could maintain
the value of their exports in terms of the industrial products they required in
exchange from the oil consumers.

The successful inauguration of the White Revolution brought with it changes in
the political system. In December 1963 the two-party system was reorganized to
the extent that the Nationalists lapsed and a new party, Iran-i Novin (New Iran),
became the dominant government party, though for a time other opposition parties
continued to exist. In January 1965 the leader of this party, 'Abbas Huvaida, became Prime Minister, a post he was to hold for twelve years before yielding to a
younger man, Jamshid Amuzgar – a striking expression of the new-found stability
and unity in a country that had been used to changes of government almost
annually. The new spirit of unity was also symbolized in 1976 by the introduction
of a one-party system, under which all political groupings were incorporated into
the single Rastakhiz-i Iran (Resurrection of Iran) Party, within which differences
of opinion were provided for by the organization of party 'wings'. These measures
to give the general population a greater share in the evolution of government
policy did not disguise the fact that the driving force behind all these reforms
continued to be the Shah himself. By 1967 the process of reconstruction and
resettlement of the country had gone far enough for the formal ceremony of
coronation, which had been impossible in the wartime conditions of his accession
twenty-six years earlier, to be celebrated in the presence of an international gathering. Four years later the largest gathering of heads of state ever to be assembled in
one place witnessed, at the tomb of Cyrus the Great in the south of Iran, the com-
memoration of the 2,500th anniversary of the foundation of the Persian monarchy
by that ruler and of the first declaration of the rights of man. Though Iran had
seen many vicissitudes of fortune since that time, yet the celebration was a legitimate
recognition of the fact that Iran had never been conquered spiritually, and had

always in the end absorbed her conquerors while retaining her own integrity. It was a fitting epilogue to this event that in 1976 the Iranian calendar, which till then had, in spite of the change in 1924 from lunar to solar reckoning, continued to be dated from the Moslem Hijra in AD622, was changed to date from the accession of Cyrus to the throne in 559BC. This was not a slight on the Islamic faith, but a perpetual memorial to the man whom HIM Muhammad Riza Shah Pahlavi thus addressed on 13th October 1971:

'After the passage of twenty-five centuries, the Iranian flag is flying today as triumphantly as it flew in thy glorious age. The name of Iran today evokes as much respect throughout the world as it did in thy days. Today, as in thy age, Iran bears the message of liberty and the love of mankind in a troubled world, and is the guardian of the loftiest human aspirations. The torch thou kindledst has for two thousand five hundred years never died in spite of the storms of history. Today it casts its light upon this land more brightly than ever and, as in thy time, its brilliance spreads far beyond the boundaries of Iran.'

ABOVE
The dying hero Rustam shoots his treacherous brother Shaghad. Mid 14th century. From the 'Demotte' *Shahnameh*
British Museum OA 1948–12–11–025
By courtesy of the Trustees of the British Museum

BELOW
Rustam slays the demon Arzhang. Shiraz, c 1433–35. From the *Shahnameh* of Ibrahim Sultan *Bodleian Library MS Ouseley Add. 176, f.70a*
By courtesy of the Curators of the Bodleian Library, Oxford

بسی شب بمستی نشد وبخودی
گذاریم یکروز در بخردی

یک امروز بنیم در ماه ومهر
کشایم سر بستهای سپهر

بدانیم کین چرخ کارگاه پشت
چگونه در آمد نجاک در بشت

3

Persian Literature

P. W. AVERY

The aesthetic and intellectual delight of mankind has been greatly enhanced by
Persian literature, the poetry especially. 'Persian' because, though the land is Iran,
the language is *Farsi*, Persian. The prose and poetry of the Islamic epoch have been
written in New Persian, whose emergence as an incomparable vehicle of poetry may
be dated from very early poets such as Hanzala of Badghis and Muhammad ibn
Vasif, the latter flourishing as late as AD900. Like the fugitive reference in the Arabic
Kitab al-Aghani ('Book of Songs') to how one Silmak put a snatch into Persian
from Arabic in the days of Harun al-Rashid (786–809), these poets' fragments
point to an early and gradual birth of a great tradition, to be demonstrated in an
astonishing degree of completed development in the work of Rudaki, who died in
AD940–1.

Scholarship has not so far established any substantial documentary link between
this New Persian poetry of some two centuries after the fall of Iran's last pre-Islamic
rulers, the Sasanids, and expression in song or hymn, verse or psalm, of the epochs
of Middle and Old Persian. Although, as the hint in the 'Book of Songs' shows, the

Iskandar (Alexander the Great) and the Seven Sages. Herat, 1495. From the *Khamseh* of Nizami.
By Bihzad
British Library Or. 6810, f. 214a
By courtesy of the British Library Board

beginnings of that Persian poetry which has so signally enriched the culture of man-kind must have been earlier than was for long supposed.

Documentary evidence may always elude us. That a tradition of minstrelsy existed under the Sasanids is known. It seems self-evident that during the 'two centuries of silence' following the advent of the Arabs in 641 songs continued to be sung in praise of sweethearts, of wine, and perhaps in the evocative and sad strain characteristic of later pieces. They were not written down. 'Pahlavi' continued in various spoken dialects; but as Arab governors were appointed from Damascus, later Baghdad, to areas which included Iran's remotest provinces, Arabic spread as the written medium. Scribes, courtiers and legists, men turned Muslim and therefore dependent upon the Arabic *Quran* for devotional and juridical guidance, had to master the reading and writing of the language of their new masters from Arabia.

The Old Persian of the Achaemenians, preserved in inscriptions; Avestan; Median; Parthian, and the Pahlavi dialects of the period 300BC to AD900 and comprising Middle Persian, had all, with the exception of the last, long since been transmuted and in their original forms quite forgotten. Pahlavi numerical notations survived in the hands of the Arabs' Iranian secretaries and book-keepers, indeed texts were written in Pahlavi, too, for many years after the advent of Islam and the Arabs; but Arabic as the language of administration, religion and literature ultimately prevailed. When a written new form of Persian arose, with only slight modifications its alphabet was Arabic.

Thus Iran's ancient literary forms of expression remained, petrified, uncompre-hended, on the rocks or tablets where a Darius or a Xerxes had commanded their commemorative inscriptions to be carved. They awaited the aptitude of 19th century scholars to discover what 'Saith Darius the King' of his consolidation of a great empire; or how Xerxes recorded his accession, his own 'much excellent construction' and 'protection of what had been built by my Father'.

After the 7th century translations were made out of Pahlavi into Arabic and the tradition of this 'book' dialect lingered. That nevertheless Middle Persian was superseded must be ascribed to more than the change of religion from Zoroastrianism to Islam. Firstly, Pahlavi or Middle Persian is a heading for several not so much dialects, but languages or forms of language for different classes of people and different occasions; and the priestly caste held the key to the written form. This variety of speech – ceremonial, court, royal for members of the imperial family among themselves, sacerdotal, for the hunting field, and for uttering petitions – crumbled before the ubiquitousness and relative simplicity of Arabic. Secondly, the alphabet of the written form was a borrowed dress that made understanding the phonemes for which its Aramaic-derived symbols stood a difficult, esoteric business.

This, however cursorily, is to describe the disappearance from men's understanding of speech in its most sophisticated, artificial and merely scriptorial guises. The vitality of Persian literature and the beautiful viability of Persian today, as in the 9th century, prove how the lips of a conquered people must have gone on using and fashioning their own distinctive speech, so that its essence and the dynamic of its development into a subtle and varied instrument of expression suffered no break in continuity. More, the spoken language of Iranians who so cleverly mastered Arabic that soon they were adding lustre to the Arabic poetry of ʿAbbasid Baghdad, apparently already by the 9th century afforded a pliant and variable enough bed of syntactical possibility to be capable of receiving deliberate and skilful enrichment by the incorporation of Arabic words, over and above those which would come naturally to the pens of bilingual composers who strove for the fullest attainable means of expression.

Among the Arabs, poetry was most highly prized. A passport to acceptance, honour and fame, skill in it could ensure status for those who, perhaps fugitives from another tribe, perhaps star-struck because of their peculiar talent, might not otherwise have fitted into any of the normal patterns of a closely organized and thrifty tribal society. The status thus conferred was, moreover, one of influence; few people are more susceptible to the power of rhetoric than the Arabs. As it was, after the Arab conquest a system of clientage had to be evolved to accommodate those Iranians who chose to work with the Arabs, into the Arab social structure. Therefore, it is not surprising that some Iranians were quick to perceive the openings afforded in the Arab ethos to the dexterous rhymester. They achieved prominence in the first place as poets in Arabic. Then in such centres of the new Perso-Arabic civilization as the cities of Bukhara and Samarqand, the practice arose of making imitations of Arabic verse in Persian. In less highly cultured conditions, as for example those characteristic of the entourage of Yaʿqub ibn Lais, who wrested independence from the Arabs in 867 in south-eastern Iran, Persian was substituted for Arabic as the language of poetry simply because the Amir asked for verses in his praise to be in a language which he understood. Muhammad ibn Vasif obeyed the command and left on record one of the first known pieces of Persian poetry.

As Arab dominion in the 9th century changed from direct rule, through governors sent from Baghdad, and became a federative system with local Iranian dynasts owing a loose allegiance to the Caliphs, Persian poets began increasingly to write in their own vernacular, side by side with the continuation of Arabic verse, whose prosody the Persians modified to suit their own purposes. The vine and the cupbearer appeared as new themes, and at Bukhara the Court of the Samanids (874–999) rang to the sound of the harp accompanying the voices of professional minstrels:

> *The harp's voice, sad with grief for the rose, raised a lament,*
> *Dishevelled its hair, dug finger nails into its face.*

> *Sometimes the bottle falls in prayer on to the prayer-mat:*
> *Sometimes through grief it pours out a draught from a bleeding heart.*

It was a complex hedonism, duly informed with a sense of doom, of honour and of a Power beyond that of men. Shahid of Balkh (fl 914–943) said:

> *Oh God how begrudging you seem to me because,*
> *Though priceless, yet for you there is a price to pay.*

> *Without you let no store of wealth be mine;*
> *The permitted way is thus to be lamenting, sad because of you.*

> *For the man of letters letters are army enough;*
> *Though he is with a legion the dunce remains alone.*

The prince of these earlier poets was Rudaki; and such was their awareness of the majesty and power of poetry that Shahid could see it as on a level with religious prophecy:

> *Poets' verses become part of people's speech;*
> *But for Rudaki – his speech is the recital of Revelation:*
> *For poets 'well done!' and 'bravo!' are praise.*
> *For Rudaki, 'well done!' and 'bravo!' would be mockery.*

They set the stage upon which Firdausi (died 1021) was, in about 980, to begin his long epic march, in the *mutaqarib* metre, ∪ - - / ∪ - - / ∪ - - / ∪ -, with a variation of / ∪ - - / ∪ - - / ∪ - - / ∪ - ∪ /, gathering together in some 60,000 couplets the legends of Iran, to form the *Shahnameh*, ('The Book of Kings'). His verses were the stirring drum-beat of the great poem, at once the glorification of Iran, Iranians' courage and love of truth and of colour, and the lament, conceived in nostalgia, for an Iran overcome by military despots from further Asia. The lavish rewards bestowed upon Rudaki and other Court poets of the period, and that of the Ghaznavid rulers which succeeded it, was an incentive to divert the attention of Persian scholars from Baghdad to various centres in Iran and to the Persian language as the vehicle of expression. By 1010, when Firdausi was drawing his work to an end, the Samanids were no more. Their erstwhile military slaves had founded a dynasty in Ghazna, to whose Mahmud the poet presented his work. The reception was not all that it might have been.

Never mind: another, and the largest, fabric in Persian speech had been created, to assist the process of establishing the language, at times, in a history full of catastrophe, to seem to be all that the Iranian people had to hold on to as evidence of their never entirely eclipsed identity. Firdausi's *Shahnameh* has also remained a reminder of the possibility of national unity and greatness. It has been the inspiration of all generations of Iranians down to the present-day and has served to hold the nation together in the memory of shared legends about shared sufferings and glories. Besides the vicissitudes from without, regionalism within such an extensive realm as the Persian was a factor, and it is interesting to see how, once its poetry became famous, the Persian of the north-east was deliberately purveyed to other parts of the country. Dictionaries, of which one remains, were compiled to help poets elsewhere to evaluate accurately the vocabulary of the Samanid pace-setting poets. Nasir-i Khusrau tells how, in about 1045, he helped Qatran of Tabriz better to understand the collected works of Manjik and Daqiqi. This was more than a matter of archaisms; it was to establish a durable and universally comprehended vehicle of expression, the cement of nationhood.

There was the zest for novelty, first in the language itself; then in the art of penning it; finally, the quest for novelty in striking off new and startling images whereby to move afresh the heart and titillate the mind in taking up perennial and basic human topics, of love, separation, sorrow and joy. That penmanship, resulting in calligraphic sumptuousness always to be associated with Persian literature, was in itself a source of joy is witnessed by 'Unsuri (died 1038–1040) the Ghaznavid poet:

The knot of pitch placed on the silver page:
Chain mail painted with musk on the almond blossom,

and 'the silver page' reminds us of the introduction to Samarqand from China of paper, and the continuing care and improvement in its manufacture, of which old Persian manuscripts afford evidence.

Nasir-i Khusrau described his encounter with Qatran in the simplest prose – 'In Tabriz I saw a poet, name, Qatran. He used to compose poetry well. Only he did not know Persian well. He came to me . . .' The early prose was of this simple, laconic order. Under the Ghaznavids a return to Arabic examples accompanied a revival of religious formalism. Persian prose became 'Augustanly' Arabicized; but works like *The History of the Ghaznavids* by Abul Fazl Baihaqi (11th century), Nizam al-Mulk's *Treatise on Government* (1091–92) and the *Qabus Nameh* ('A Mirror for Princes') of 1082, were of sufficient directness and hardness of diction to serve as a model for 20th century prose-writers who sought language having the dignity of literature, but also the clarity and ring of the spoken word.

Sa'di, as well as being a great poet, brought Persian prose of the high Islamic period to the apogee of perfection, albeit in an intricately stylized form of rhyming prose. Artificial yes, but perfect enough for the art to be concealed, the ear, eye and mind delighted by the graceful convolutions through which, with such seeming ease, Sa'di puts that thoroughbred, the Persian Language, which he so completely commanded. Born between 1213 and 1219, Sa'di of Shiraz adopted one of the oldest features of Persian literature, the moral tale. In verse and prose, notably in products of his early middle-age (1257 and 1258), *Bustan* ('The Orchard') and *Gulistan* ('The Flower Garden'), he inculcated magnanimity, especially in tyrants, repentance, tolerance and other virtues through the artifice of entertaining and easily memorized poems and prose anecdotes. His life-time spanned the Mongol invasions: he gathered up and reincarnated the shocked and shattered wisdom and refinement of Iranian civilization. Among his contemporaries were annalists, such as the historian of Hülegü's conquest of Iran, Juvaini (died 1283), whose task was to preserve a record for posterity of what Iran had suffered and survived. Sa'di brought back to literature the abstract and contemplative; the fruits of experience objectively set forth for men to ponder and ameliorate their actions by.

His fellow-citizen of Shiraz, Hafiz (died 1390), used the instrument of the lyric, *ghazal*, he inherited from Sana'i (died 1130–1131) and which had been skilfully continued by Sa'di, to carry much of the imagery and pointedness of which Rudaki and the earlier poets gave him the example, and to spellbind his contemporaries, and all of subsequent epochs and many nations who have been fascinated by the finest poetry known to man. Hafiz's *ghazals*, susceptible, like Scripture, to interpretation on many different levels, also have the appeal of a song, simply to please their auditor or reader.

While Sa'di lived one who as a child had been taken away from lands stricken by the Mongols composed in distant Anatolia the great text of Persian mysticism, a tapestry of allegories about human deprivation of the greatest of human needs, apprehension of God, and about how this aching separation and desolation may be bridged, so that the contentment and freedom of living in God are achieved. Rumi died in 1273, having in his *Masnavi* brought to fullness the spiritual and allegorical literature of which Sana'i and 'Attar had earlier been exponents, when social and political hardships had led the people of Iran increasingly to seek the solace of the inner life.

The lyrical and mystical traditions attained another flowering in the 15th century, in the poetry of Jami. Jami inherited both a development of the epic strain beyond the use to which Firdausi had put it, and the long episodic allegorical poem perfected by 'Attar and woven into a vast corpus by Jalal al-Din Rumi. The epic development ready to Jami's hand was that accomplished by Nizami in the last half of the 12th century. No survey of Persian literature would be just that did not pay homage to Nizami of Ganja. He incidentally represents, if one thinks back a moment to the ever present regional aspect of the history and development of Persian literature, the as it were Irano-Christian enclave of the Caucasian area, which was adorned also by Khaqani, master of the panegyric and elegiac odes as well as a renowned sonneteer, born some thirty-three years before Nizami's demise.

Nizami altered the epic from the 'factual' narrative of legendary episodes which it is in the *Shahnameh*, to make it present episodes as symbols, heroes as paragons, so that the whole mechanism of the epic was lifted on to a more abstract level, and a strong spiritual element introduced. His power as limner of scenes was such that his descriptions have a quality of atmosphere and colour, the huntsman, the girl, the cheetah, the horses, plain and sky being brought so alive on to the page, that inevitably his 'Five Books', the *Khamseh*, works which influenced Jami in his *Sab'eh*, became the inspiration of the miniaturist: to Nizami's words the visual art of Iran owes a very great deal. To him Jami owed the example of the ethical-philosophical poem, while Jami the Sufi naturally also fell under the influence of 'Attar and Rumi.

In fact Jami was so prolific and, as skilled in all branches of his art as he was steeped in the works of his long line of predecessors, so apt in drawing on the resources of Persian poetry, that he inevitably resuscitated the high tradition after the sufferings and chaos of Timur's invasions. He also became this tradition's exporter: his works, in superb manuscripts in a world to which printing was not introduced until the 19th century, were eagerly purchased by the Sultans and wealthy Pashas of the Ottoman Turkish empire, where the modes and crafts of Turkish literature were thoroughly imbued with the Persian taste.

Jami, however, was not only the reviver of a great tradition, but also its concluder, for his death in 1492 is a terminal point. The history of Persian poetry is punctuated by periods when political and social conditions made the maintaining of the tradition in its higher forms impossible. Its persistence in spite of this is due to the way in which, on times becoming more propitious, men of letters consciously gathered together what remained from the past and recollected the various literary manifestations of their civilization in, to cite only one example, works such as Daulatshah's *Memoirs of the Poets*. These works were really anthologies, biographical notices of the composers being interspersed among quotations from their works; often the only vestiges of a poet's creations extant are those which have come down to us in books of this kind and in manuals on the art of poetry. Daulatshah died in about 1494; he was Jami's contemporary. A late example, his work is not dissimilar to Jami's own memoirs of the great Sufi Saints, 'The Fragrant Breezes of Good Fellowship'. Both works stem from a long tradition of this type of recollective writing, collations made lest in the revolutions of time men should forget the great exemplars of the spiritual life and of the canons of literary creativity. Daulatshah had predecessors in Nizami the Prosodist, who was a friend of 'Omar Khayyam and wrote in 1156; and 'Aufi, who compiled his recollections of poets in 1221 and called it 'The Quintessence of Hearts'. As the biographer of saints Jami had among his predecessors the Arabic writer Sulami and the Persian mystic, Jami's fellow townsman of Herat, Ansari, who died in 1088.

It is evident that the obverse of great reversals of fortune was an uninhibited capacity to return to models of long before, tenaciously to revive very old traditions, their value the more highly esteemed because, through ages when so much was lost and destroyed, they were all that was of real value left. In Persian literature to draw on ancient precedents was not simply a slavish repetition. The tapping of old springs was always accompanied by the addition of fresh ideas and deployment of new strokes of ingenuity. Though Jami's death is generally taken to mark the end of these periodic revivals of the high tradition, this tradition cannot in fact be said ever to have quite died. Later poets have certainly proved themselves gifted exponents and, as will be seen below, 'rebels' against the diction of the Safavid era, who in some instances advocated returning to the traditional style of poets before the time of Jami; it must be said that Qa'ani, who died in 1854, and Bahar, who died in 1951, both resorted to it.

The victories in 1502 of Isma'il the Safavid inaugurated a political consolidation and a new religious coherence in Iran; but the Safavid era's lustre rests chiefly in architecture and the visual and decorative arts, not in the literary. The efforts of the educated writer were channelled into the construction of a religious propaganda and into preparing manuals of religious conduct. These writers were often men who thought in Arabic and knew Persian only imperfectly. The Shahs, though interested in poetry, were apt to be exponents of it in Turkish, the language which they generally spoke, and not in Persian. The lower traditions of speech, however, continued a lively and racy existence. Lampoons and ballad poetry were never wanting, while the more classical expression declined into artificiality and became encrusted with superfluity that was not to be corrected, in prose as well as poetry, until the 19th and 20th centuries. Qa'ani emerged as a master in the poetic field and the reforming Minister, Qa'im Maqam Farahani (1779–1835), began the task of making Persian prose a fitting vehicle for use in the modern world.

From the opening of the 19th century Iran became increasingly involved in a new range of diplomatic relations, principally with the European powers. Men like

Qa'im Maqam Farahani and his enlightened successor Mirza Taqi Khan were compelled to develop a prose suitable for the conduct of diplomatic negotiations. Modification in officialese opened the way for modifications in other spheres of writing. The political theorists of the early 20th century were not only observant of European technological advances but also conversant with European languages and liberal political ideas. For them the older style of prose writing was a matter for jest. Dehkhuda, who died in 1955, first came into prominence as a literary figure when he parodied the old conventions. But the mockery was in dead earnest. The situation from which 20th century Persian writers had to escape was one in which subservience to high-flown and out-worn clichés constituted a strait-jacket on freedom of expression. Writing with the direct comprehensibility of the spoken word was ruled out. Moreover, the scribe's calling had inevitably become a specialized function open only to a few initiates, men whose own poverty in ideas made them accept constrictions easily, while they equally readily accepted and perpetuated the notion, in which they had a vested interest, that the spoken word was not respectable enough to be put into writing.

Pithy comment on social and political conditions could still be made, in softly recited satires in verse, whose applause took the form of quiet chuckles from the members of intimate gatherings. This was not enough for reformers who had compelling reasons to communicate loudly and clearly to all and sundry, to educate their beloved but backward compatriots in new ways and discoveries. Printing had come, and so had the newspaper. Prose was bound to undergo profound changes. Thus the way was open for the short story and novel writers of the mid-20th century, as well as the essayists, the work of them all pioneered in the nineteen-twenties by the stories of Sayyid Muhammad 'Ali Jamalzadeh and by the scholarly articles published in a journal such as *Kaveh*, printed in Berlin.

During the 19th century and the first two decades of the 20th century Persian literature entered a period of revolt against the stereotyped diction of the Safavid era, when literary accomplishment was taken as the use of far-fetched conceits drawn from the experience of everyday life and expressed in the language of the day seasoned with Arabic phrases and idioms.

In the first phase of the revolt the rebels advocated a return to the traditional style of the great poets, with some emphasis upon the use of pure Persian words or the Arabic words which had become acclimatized and lost their lineage and foreign flavour. Qa'ani and Visal of Shiraz and his sons, and Surush of Isfahan, Saba of Kashan, Adib al-Mamalik of Farahan, and Danish of Tehran were the fore-runners of this group.

The second phase of the revolt, which is still active, followed the same principles, but, influenced by their knowledge of European literature, the new generation of rebels introduced unity of theme in their descriptive poetry or poems composed on the social and political events of the time. To this group belong Bahar, Iraj of Tehran, 'Arif of Qazvin, Suratgar of Shiraz and Khanlari together with the great poetess of modern Iran, Parvin I'tisami.

The ultra modern poetry owes its existence and a new vitality to such men as Nima of Yushij, Tavalluli of Shiraz and Nadir Nadirpur.

Authors in prose, Hidayat, Jalal Al-Ahmad, Chubak, to name only a few, have taken as their themes the misery of the poor, the *ennui* of provincial life, the anxieties of the village school-master, the tensions of a society in transition with the unavoidable clash between the different generations. The modern element in their work is the evidence of an increasing preoccupation with the effects of experience upon the individual. In this these writers are in line with modern writers everywhere. They have laid aside the more abstract universal criteria that were the stock-in-trade of earlier writers. Hence for their purposes prose rather than poetry is the right medium. And yet, as one sees in the opening pages of 'Ali Dashti's *Fitna* and the *Prison Days*, and 'Alavi's *Scattered Pages in Prison*, this modern Persian prose has a musical quality inalienable from poetic utterance in the Persian language; while Sadiq Chubak writes as if to hint to the miniaturist in the tradition of Persian pictorial art that the scenes he describes in words might equally well be delineated in the miniature. Jalal Al-Ahmad shows the same loving care over detail as Chubak, but in such of his more, and justly, celebrated works as *The School Principal*, life is portrayed in the psychology of his chief characters: rather than in sketches of the background it is human speech and the facets of the human mind that lead us into the situations this remarkable writer would make his words vividly and poignantly capture. He and 'Alavi certainly prove what a crucible of human experience Iran can be and how persistently strong Iranian genius can remain in expressing this experience.

The innovators in poetry and prose of the period up to 1950 have been followed by writers who have continued using and developing the new styles in a manner that has further consolidated and established them, making their acceptance by fresh generations assured. Ghulam Husain Sa'idi is an example of a young writer who has profited from experience in the Government Literacy Corps' campaign against illiteracy in rural areas: he has given us his *Qissehha-yi-Rusta* ('Rural Tales') as well as a volume of verse. Ahmad Shamlu, Akhavaneh Salis, Farrukhzad and Ni'mat Mirzazadeh have made their names as poets.

However modern and original these authors, their great heritage is nevertheless continually evident. The heirs of a tradition that might have overwhelmed and stifled them, their courage has not failed them: they have not felt that there was no scope left for further invention. Like those of the past the modern writers have not been afraid to return to the old springs. It is happy that they are found to be as interesting and satisfying as their precursors of a thousand years.

4

Persian Painting

B. W. ROBINSON

Pre-Islamic Persian painting is virtually unknown to us, though we do know that it existed. It seems likely that in spite of the Arab conquest and the subsequent centuries of alien rule, native traditions persisted. Some of the figures on Nishapur pottery of the 10th to 11th centuries, for example, have a markedly Sasanian character. Such examples of Persian book-painting as there may have been at this time, however, were swept away in the Mongol cataclysm of the early 13th century which culminated in the sack of Baghdad in 1258.

Baghdad itself had been, for at least half a century (and probably much longer), the centre of a school of book-painting of which a number of examples have survived. But, though it may be that some of the painters were Persians by birth, the school, which has sometimes been called the International 'Abbasid School, was Arab rather than Persian in character, and its artists, so far as we know, only illustrated works in the Arabic language.

For Persian painting proper we have to wait until the end of the 13th century, when the Mongol conquerors had settled down, become good Muslims, and adopted the civilization of the land they had overrun. The earliest examples we know were produced in the north-west, at Maragheh and Tabriz, and the style is a strange mixture of native tradition with ideas and techniques borrowed from Byzantium and China. The vast Mongol conquests had greatly facilitated communications. The Yüan Emperors of China were themselves Mongols; Byzantine ideas had already influenced the International 'Abbasid School of Baghdad; the

Mongols even established contacts with western Europe, and mediaeval Italian drawings were certainly known to them (copies exist in the Istanbul albums).

From this melting-pot emerged the style known to us from the early 14th century manuscripts of the World History of Rashid al-Din preserved at Edinburgh University and the Royal Asiatic Society. These miniatures are strong – one might almost say stark – and colour is very restrained. Western influence is seen in the rendering of figures and drapery, but the vegetation and landscape elements derive directly from China; compositions are simple. The miniatures are usually of narrow oblong shape with the figures disposed in a row in a single plane.

If we may believe Dust Muhammad, a court painter of the 16th century and virtually our only literary source for this period, it was in the next generation during the reign of Abu Sa'id (d 1335) that the true style of Persian painting was born of the genius of the artist Ahmad Musa. Some miniatures attributed to him in the Istanbul albums bear out Dust Muhammad's statement, which was no doubt the oral tradition current among court artists of his time. Though it has been usual to discredit these admittedly later attributions, the tradition may well be worthy of more credit than it has sometimes received; the attributions, in fact, appear to date from about the period when Dust Muhammad wrote his valuable account. He goes on to tell us that Ahmad Musa's pupil Shams al-Din was the chief illustrator of a great *Shahnameh* manuscript executed for the Jalayirid Sultan Uvais (1356–75), and it seems reasonable here to follow Mr Eric Schroeder in equating this latter manuscript with the celebrated 'Demotte *Shahnameh*', of which many miniatures survive in the great collections of England, France, and the United States.

From all this it seems clear that what Ahmad Musa did was to blend the heterogeneous and ill-digested foreign elements of early 14th century painting, to develop a rich colour-scheme, and to expand the compositions. Even in the Demotte *Shahnameh*, however, we find a number of miniatures which are still fairly close to the Rashid al-Din illustrations of 1306–14, presumably the work of an elderly artist trained in the school of Rashidiyya. But the majority are far more advanced, and show us that by this time Persian painting as we know it was well and truly launched, though its Mongol-Chinese character was still very marked. It may be mentioned here that all through the history of Persian painting we frequently find, side-by-side in the same manuscript, works that appear archaic and others in which new ideas and developments are evident. All the great royal manuscripts were illustrated by groups of artists amongst whom there must always have been at least one middle-aged or elderly man of senior standing but old-fashioned ideas, who belonged to the previous generation and was too set in his ways to follow the new trends. His achieved reputation gave him an honoured place amongst his younger and more progressive colleagues, and he was often entrusted with the double-page frontispiece or other important miniatures in the set. As examples may be quoted the painter of the first miniature in the Chester Beatty Library Amir Khusrau of 1485; Mirak of Khurasan, Bihzad's teacher, in the British Museum Nizami of 1494; Sadiq, the painter of 'Zal and the Simurgh' in the fragmentary *Shahnameh* of Shah 'Abbas I in the Chester Beatty Library; Malik Husain Isfahani in the Windsor *Shahnameh* of 1648; and Mu'in *musavvir* in the New York *Shahnameh* of 1693. It is not always necessary to feel uneasy if all the miniatures in a manuscript are not entirely homogeneous in style.

By the end of the 14th century the Jalayirid court style under the patronage of Sultan Ahmad had still further refined on the developed style of the Demotte *Shahnameh*. The paintings of Junaid, a pupil of Shams al-Din, in the British Museum Khwaju Kirmani of 1396 give us at last the pure Persian style we associate with the 15th century, the golden age of the Timurids. It had already spread beyond Baghdad, the Jalayirid capital, and we find it in a primitive and provincial, but nevertheless unmistakable form, in several manuscripts illustrated under the Muzaffarid rulers of Shiraz between about 1370 and 1393, when the city was taken by Timur.

In order to trace the course of the main stream of Persian painting – the Metropolitan Court Style, as we shall call it – we must now consider the Timurid successors of the Jalayirid sultans Uvais and Ahmad as patrons of fine book-production. Among Timur's immediate descendants we find the young prince Iskandar Sultan, who while still in his 'teens had already deputized for his father, Timur's second son 'Umar Shaikh, as governor of Shiraz. Although his political career was extremely stormy until his final fall in 1415, Iskandar found time to indulge a passion for fine manuscripts which had developed in boyhood, if we are right in supposing that the collection of epics of 1397 now divided between the British Museum and the Chester Beatty Library was executed under his patronage. But the greatest monuments to his taste are the Gulbenkian Anthology of 1410 and the British Museum Miscellany of a year or so later. It seems not unlikely that he had taken over some of the Jalayirid court artists and that they contributed to these magnificent volumes.

After the downfall of Iskandar Sultan his mantle as the foremost patron of painting fell upon Baisunghur Mirza, another grandson of Timur, who acted as governor of Herat for his father Shah Rukh from 1415 till his early death in 1433. The centre of the metropolitan court style thus moved from Shiraz and Yazd to the north-eastern capital of Herat where Baisunghur set up an academy of book-production, gathering a large staff of calligraphers, painters, gilders, binders, and illuminators from all over the Timurid dominions. His leading calligrapher Ja'far was appointed director of this establishment, and among the splendid manuscripts produced there under Baisunghur's patronage it is sufficient to mention the Chester Beatty *Gulistan* of 1426, the Istanbul *Kalileh va Dimneh* of 1430, and the Tehran *Shahnameh* of 1431. Under Baisunghur's guidance the style was standardized and, if possible, still further refined. In fact a little of the freshness of the earlier work done for Iskandar Sultan was lost. The highest standards of execution were always insisted on, and Baisunghuri miniatures glow with the colour and precision of the finest jewels.

For about thirty-five years after the young prince's death there was no outstanding patron, though fine work was certainly done for some of the surviving Timurid

ABOVE LEFT
The Fire Ordeal of Siyavush. Herat, *c* 1440.
From the *Shahnameh* of Muhammad Juki .
Royal Asiatic Society MS 239, f. 76a
By courtesy of the Royal Asiatic Society
Deposited on loan to the British Library

BELOW LEFT
Portrait of Prince Imam Quli Mirza, *'Imad al-Dauleh* (1815–75), by Sani' al-Mulk, *c* 1855
British Library Or. 4938 No. 7
By courtesy of the British Library Board

RIGHT
Seated youth. Isfahan, *c* 1590–1600. By Riza
Colnaghi, Persian and Mughal Art (1976) *No. 40*
By courtesy of Colnaghi, 14 Old Bond Street,
London W1

princes such as Muhammad Juki, Ulugh Beg, and Abu Saʿid. But the days of Timurid dominion in western and central Persia were numbered; the Turcomans were pressing in from the west and the confused situation is reflected in several manuscripts from the middle years of the 15th century in which we find miniatures of the metropolitan court style side-by-side with others in the style that had been developed at Shiraz, and in a new and uncomplicated style that seems to have come in with the Turcomans. These manuscripts were probably produced under early Turcoman patronage.

At the same time that Baisunghur was installed at Herat by his father, his brother Ibrahim Sultan was given the governorship of Fars with its capital of Shiraz. Ibrahim too was a lover of fine books, being himself a calligrapher of repute, but he found that the best academic talent had been monopolized by his brother. However, under his patronage the painters of Shiraz evolved a style of their own, bolder, larger, and simpler than the glossy meticulous work of Baisunghur's academy, with larger figures, a more sombre colour-scheme, and not such a high finish. This style owed something, it seems, to the Muzaffarid style which, as we have seen, was practised in Shiraz before its conquest by Timur. Some of its best examples can be found in the magnificent but sadly damaged and repainted copy of the *Shahnameh* made for Ibrahim Sultan himself, which is now one of the treasures of the Bodleian Library.

After this prince's death the style seems to have contracted its scale and softened its impact. The large number of Shiraz manuscripts dating from the middle years of the 15th century (none of them of 'royal' quality) seems to indicate that the city was assuming the role of purveyor of illustrated manuscripts on a commercial scale to patrons of less than royal or noble rank. That these manuscripts were often exported is also suggested by the fact that when miniatures executed in Turkey or India are most Persian in appearance, it is always the Shiraz style of the time that they most closely resemble.

Iskandar's portrait prepared for Queen Qaidafeh (Candace). By Muhammad Qasim, 1648
Royal Library, Windsor Castle, MS Holmes 151 (Shahnameh)
By gracious permission of Her Majesty Queen Elizabeth II

The Turcomans took Shiraz in 1456, and the Shiraz-Timurid style rapidly disappeared, being replaced by the Turcoman style, a simplified and in some ways primitive 'utility' type of painting admirably adapted to the commercial role that Shiraz had apparently assumed in the field of book-production. Manuscripts illustrated in the Turcoman style are particularly numerous between about 1475 and 1500, and the Safavid style of Shiraz grew imperceptibly out of it during the first two decades of the following century. But parallel with this commercial style, a court style of great refinement was also developed under the patronage of the Turcoman princes, especially Pir Budaq, during the middle years of the 15th century. This is best exemplified in two notable manuscripts, the Tehran *Kalileh va Dimneh* of *c* 1465 (formerly dated to the early 15th century), and the Chester Beatty Tabari of 1471. At first the style owed much to Herat but later, under Ya'qub Beg at Tabriz, it became more fantastic, and freer in both colour and drawing, reaching its apogee in his Nizami of 1481 in the Topkapi Library at Istanbul (H 762).

Meanwhile Herat remained the centre of the metropolitan court style, receiving a fresh impetus from the enlightened and enthusiastic patronage of Sultan Husain Mirza, the last great Timurid prince, who ruled there from 1468 till his death in 1506. By 1480 Sultan Husain's court was adorned by a bright constellation of poets, historians, musicians, and architects, and it was at about this time that Kamal al-Din Bihzad, generally acknowledged to be the greatest of all Persian painters, added still further lustre to it. Working always within the well-established canons of Persian painting, he softened and naturalized its academic rigour; his figures are individuals, his trees and plants appear often to have been drawn from life, his line is more fluid, and his grouping and composition free and balanced without rigid symmetry. He was a reformer, not a revolutionary. It has already been noticed how we often find in some of the best manuscripts brilliant progressive miniatures side-by-side with others which, though of equally brilliant execution, still follow the canons of a previous generation. An excellent example of this is the celebrated British Museum Nizami of 1494, executed for the Amir 'Ali Farsi Barlas. The majority of the miniatures are by Bihzad himself or artists of his circle following his style, but the double-page frontispiece and two or three other compositions are by his teacher, Mirak, who continued to produce exquisite work, but with the rather rigid figure drawing and grouping and the formal vegetation of the age of Baisunghur.

When the Safavid dynasty came to power at the beginning of the 16th century, Bihzad was well on in middle age, but his high reputation caused Shah Isma'il to appoint him director of the royal library staff in 1522. He seems to have done very little painting in his latter years. Meanwhile a new and brilliant generation of young artists was spreading its wings under the munificent patronage of the youthful Shah Tahmasp (acc 1524), who had himself been taught the art by Sultan Muhammad, the senior member of this group of court painters. Other prominent figures were Mirak, who became Tahmasp's favourite painter (not, of course, to be confused with the elder Mirak of Khurasan, Bihzad's teacher), Mir *musavvir*, and his son Mir Sayyid'Ali, and their work is to be found in the two most sumptuous Persian manuscripts ever produced, the Rothschild (now Houghton) *Shahnameh*, with over 250 full-size miniatures, and the better-known British Museum Nizami of 1539–43.

Persia being truly unified under the Safavids, the metropolitan court style naturally moved with the capital of the country. This was at first Tabriz, but that city was soon found to be too vulnerable to Turkish attacks, and in 1548 the court moved to Qazvin. In his later years Shah Tahmasp lost interest in painting and became a religious bigot, but the tradition of enlightened princely patronage was maintained by his nephew Prince Ibrahim Mirza, who held his court at Mashhad. A magnificent manuscript of Jami's poems, the *Haft Aurang* or Seven Thrones, now in the Freer Gallery of Art, Washington, is the best surviving monument to the prince's taste and munificence. The text dates from between 1556 and 1565, and the miniatures admirably illustrate the transition between the Tabriz style of Tahmasp's early years and mature style of Qazvin. They are, as usual in manuscripts of the first quality, the work of several hands, and while some are almost indistinguishable stylistically from work done for Tahmasp twenty years earlier, others, presumably painted by younger and more progressive artists, show a number of modifications in figure drawing and composition. The sinuous lines of the slim, youthful figures are still further emphasized, and the enclosing frame of the miniature, over which parts of the composition had been allowed to spill from early Timurid times, is now sometimes entirely disregarded. Whilst the faces of youths and maidens are rounder and smoother than ever, those of middle-aged and elderly characters are often naturalistic to the point of caricature. The baton turban, distinguishing badge of the Safavid house in its early years, was disappearing, being replaced by a neat round turban of modest dimensions.

Muhammadi of Herat, who may have been a son of the great Sultan Muhammad, became the foremost exponent of this style, and we may be justified in placing one or two of the more progressive paintings in the Freer Jami among his early work. His fame rests mainly, however, on a number of separate album-leaves bearing sometimes fully painted miniatures, like the charming 'Lovers' in the Museum of Fine Arts, Boston, and sometimes lightly tinted drawings, such as the 'Young Dervish with a Spear' in the India Office Library. With the decline of royal patronage in Tahmasp's later years, such single sheets were becoming increasingly popular as an outlet for patrons of more modest means who could not afford a fully illustrated manuscript, but nevertheless wished to indulge a taste for fine drawing and painting.

From the style of Muhammadi developed a quite distinctive local school of painting found in Khurasan (his native province) during the latter half of the 16th century. The figure drawing is smooth, competent, and uncomplicated, very much in Muhammadi's style; background details of vegetation and architecture are as simple as possible, and the colour-scheme is often dominated by pale blue, mauve, or light olive green, which are the favourite colours for the ground. Several manuscripts illustrated in this style are dated from Herat, Bakharz, and Malan – all in Khurasan.

Another distinct local style during the first century of Safavid rule is found at Shiraz. We have seen that this city was the centre of the commercial Turcoman style at the end of the Timurid period, and the earliest painting produced there under the new dynasty is indistinguishable from the latter save in the introduction of the Safavid baton turban. Gradually, however, Shiraz work approaches the metropolitan style, though running, as it were, on a lower parallel, with generally paler tones, stiffer drawing, and a rather flat provincial appearance. The enormous number of surviving Shiraz-Safavid manuscripts indicates that the city continued and expanded its activity in the production of illustrated manuscripts of rather less than the first rank on a commercial basis. Soon after 1600 the Shiraz style merges into the metropolitan style of Isfahan.

The only other style outside the main stream that we must consider here is that practised under the Özbeg Shaibanid rulers at Bukhara. On more than one occasion in the early 16th century they captured Herat and carried off numbers of Persian artists and craftsmen across the Oxus to work for them. Their style at this time was naturally that of Bihzad, and Bukhara painting maintains this basic style unchanged, but with declining standards of drawing and composition as the 16th century proceeds. By the end of it, as can be seen in two Jami manuscripts of 1595 and 1596 in the Bodleian Library, the style had become formal and sterile almost beyond recognition.

The death of Shah Tahmasp in 1576 found the metropolitan court style in a somewhat languishing condition, despite the talent of Muhammadi, Sadiqi, and a few others. Tahmasp's successor Isma'il II determined to restore its prestige, and set about gathering a competent library staff. A brutal massacre of his brothers and cousins, including the cultivated Ibrahim Mirza, gave him command of that prince's resources in the field, and he commissioned a large copy of the *Shahnameh* which survives in a number of separated miniatures. Some of these bear the names of artists who had attained prominence at this time, such as Siyavush the Georgian and Sadiqi, but the style is not coherent, and some of the miniatures show signs of hasty execution. To maintain stylistic consistency and the highest technical standards the metropolitan court style depended on a continuous succession of enlightened royal patronage. The situation in Tahmasp's latter years – the period of his turning away from painting – was not dissimilar to that in the Timurid period between the death of Baisunghur and the accession of Sultan Husain Mirza. Miniatures of different styles appear in the same manuscript. Thus the British Museum *Garshasp Nameh* of 1573 contains paintings by the veteran Muzaffar 'Ali, a nephew and pupil of Bihzad and formerly one of Tahmasp's leading court artists, by Sadiqi, an exponent of the mature Qazvin style, by Zain al-'Abidin, who worked in the style of Shiraz, and by an anonymous artist whose work, though not of the highest quality, foreshadows the Isfahan style of twenty years later. Similarly Isma'il II's *Shahnameh* contains paintings in the styles of both Qazvin and Shiraz, as does the splendid *Shahnameh* of about 1580 in the Royal Library at Windsor.

Isma'il II reigned less than two years, and a period of political instability and confusion followed, from which Shah 'Abbas emerged supreme in 1587. Though his latter years were stained with cruelty, he deserves the epithet of 'the Great' which is usually attached to his name, and was indeed a munificent patron of painting. It seems to have been a habit of Persian rulers to commission a manuscript of the *Shahnameh*, as magnificent as their resources would allow, to celebrate their reigns. Thus we have already noted *Shahnameh* manuscripts executed for the Jalayirid Sultan Uvais, for Baisunghur and his brother Ibrahim Sultan, for Tahmasp and Isma'il II; and it is also true of the later monarchs 'Abbas II (the Leningrad *Shahnameh* of 1642–51) and Safi II (the *Shahnameh* of 1693 in the Metropolitan Museum of Art, New York). Two such manuscripts were commissioned by 'Abbas I. One, of 1614, in the New York Public Library (Spencer Collection) is a freak, being either a copy or a pastiche of a Baisunghuri manuscript, the early Timurid style being reproduced with astonishing fidelity. The other, which belongs to the very beginning of his reign and of which a portion survives in the Chester Beatty Library, is of superb quality and great splendour. The two main contributors are, firstly, Sadiqi, who was in charge of the library staff, a man of enormous talent and masterly technique (his 'Simurgh carrying the infant Zal to its nest' is one of the finest 16th century Persian miniatures in existence); and, secondly, Riza, harbinger of the new phase of the metropolitan court style which we know by the name of Isfahan, the city to which 'Abbas moved his capital in 1598.

The personality and work of Riza have been the centre of a long and sometimes heated controversy. We have, on the one hand, a group of works of superb quality, dating apparently from about 1590–1600 (amongst which are several miniatures in the Chester Beatty *Shahnameh*, as already mentioned) some of which bear the signature or attribution 'Riza' or 'Aqa Riza'; and on the other hand another group stretching as late as 1635, signed 'Riza-yi 'Abbasi'. These latter are also of high quality as a rule, but of much less delicacy than the earlier group, and characterized by a strong colour-scheme in which purple, yellow and brown are prominent. Are these two groups the work of two different men, or of the same man at different stages of his career? The arguments on both sides cannot be recapitulated here; suffice it to say that Dr Stchoukine's latest book (*Les Peintures des Manuscrits de Shah 'Abbas Ier*, 1964) leaves no doubt that the second solution is correct.

Riza was the prime mover in the new style, in which a strongly calligraphic line and the colour scheme mentioned above are the outstanding features. The figures and faces fill out after the slimness of Qazvin work, and there is often a discreet suggestion of a double-chin. But in spite of the greatness of Shah 'Abbas, the Safavid dynasty was in a state of progressive decline during the 17th century, and this is reflected in the languorous and erotic nature of many works of the Isfahan style. Riza's manner was taken up by a number of younger contemporaries such as Muhammad Qasim, Muhammad Yusuf, Afzal al-Husaini and Muhammad 'Ali, and was somewhat modified by his pupil the long-lived Mu'in, who was the best artist of the middle and later years of the 17th century. The Windsor *Shahnameh* of 1648, containing paintings by Muhammad Qasim and Muhammad Yusuf, gives an excellent idea of this phase of the Isfahan style.

But the even course of Persian painting was broken in the 1670s by the introduction of an Italianizing style by Muhammad Zaman. His works are exquisitely painted, with carefully rendered modelling of faces and drapery and a painstaking exactitude of perspective in the representation of buildings. This Europeanized style became immediately popular; Muhammad Zaman was permitted to add Italianizing miniatures to two of the finest manuscripts in the royal library, the British Museum Nizami of Shah Tahmasp and the Chester Beatty *Shahnameh* of Shah 'Abbas, and to touch up some of their original paintings. The leading court artists followed him, and we get an excellent idea of the state of the art at the end of the Safavid period from the New York *Shahnameh* of 1693. This contains 'progressive' Europeanizing work by 'Ali Naqi and Muhammad Zaman, but also, as we might expect from earlier precedents, paintings in the classic but now outdated Isfahan style, the best of which are by Riza's pupil Mu'in, who must by this time have been an old man.

The Safavid dynasty collapsed in 1722 before an invasion of the Ghilzai Afghans, and very little painting has survived from the 18th century, a period of almost continuous political turmoil. Under European influence large oil paintings (mostly portraits) were taking the place of book-painting as the most profitable and prestigious outlet for the court artists' talents; miniature painting was increasingly relegated to the decoration of lacquered caskets, bookbindings, mirror-cases, and pen-boxes. The only outstanding artist was Sadiq (fl 1740–95) in whose hands the Europeanizing manner of Muhammad Zaman and his followers was moulded into the style we generally associate with the early years of the Qajar dynasty.

The first Qajar monarch, Agha Muhammad Shah, fought his way to the throne in 1795, but was assassinated two years later. His nephew and successor Fath 'Ali Shah (1797–1834) inherited a cowed and pacified kingdom, and his striking appearance, long black beard, magnificent eyes, and wasp-like waist fed an immense personal vanity, which kept numerous court artists busy on life-size oil portraits; over twenty of these have survived. Fath 'Ali Shah's best court painters were Mirza Baba and Mihr 'Ali, specimens of whose work are in the Nigaristan Museum, Tehran. Book-painting too enjoyed a certain revival during his reign, the most splendid example being a copy of the King's own *Divan*, or collected poems, sent as a present to the Prince Regent in 1812 and now in the Royal Library at Windsor. The lacquered covers, illuminations, and marginal decorations of this sumptuous volume were the work of Mirza Baba, who also executed the two fine portraits it contains of Fath 'Ali Shah and of his uncle and predecessor, the eunuch Agha Muhammad Shah.

Much of the finest miniature painting produced under the Qajar dynasty is to be found in flower painting, lacquer and painted enamel. Muhammad Hadi (c 1730–1825) and Lutf 'Ali Khan (c 1797–1869) of Shiraz were both flower painters of exquisite skill and sensitivity. The former was interviewed as an old man by Claudius Rich, who found him 'full of the spirit of his art' and 'passionately fond of flowers'. Besides the flower paintings by which he is best known Lutf 'Ali Khan contributed some remarkable miniatures to a manuscript of the *Shahnameh* executed between 1857 and 1863 apparently for his fellow-Shirazi the poet Visal, and till recently still in the family's possession. His flower designs are sometimes executed in lacquer on book-covers. But the foremost lacquer artist of the period was Najaf, or Najaf 'Ali, of Isfahan. Between about 1815 and 1885 a large number of exquisitely painted pen-boxes and other lacquer objects were turned out by him and his three talented sons Kazim, Ja'far, and Ahmad; his younger brother Isma'il (fl c 1840–71) was also an outstanding lacquer artist. Muhammad Zaman of Shiraz, an elder contemporary of Najaf, produced some fine work in lacquer, as well as oil paintings, under Fath 'Ali Shah. It was under that monarch's patronage also that the art of painted enamel on gold and silver achieved a high distinction; some brilliant examples by 'Ali, Baqir, and Muhammad Ja'far are to be seen in the Crown Jewels Museum in Tehran. The finest of the later enamels are the work of Kazim, son of Najaf 'Ali.

In his later years the court artist Mihr 'Ali had a pupil, Abu'l-Hasan Ghaffari, who became the foremost Persian painter of the mid-nineteenth century. He was sent to Italy by Muhammad Shah to study European painting, returning shortly after the accession of Nasir al-Din Shah in 1848. During the 1850s he carried out his most important works, the large oil panels of the King and his court, now in the Archaeological Museum, Tehran, and the planning and supervision of the illustration of a stupendous six-volume Persian translation of the Arabian Nights, now in the Gulistan Imperial Library. This contains over a thousand pages of miniature painting, the work of a team of thirty-four painters. Abu'l-Hasan was given the title of Sani' al-Mulk ('Painter of the Kingdom') in 1861, and died in 1866. His many portraits are outstanding and sometimes merciless in their frank exposure of the sitter's character.

Nasir al-Din Shah was a keen patron of painting, and had some skill in drawing himself. He founded an academy of art in Tehran with the express purpose of teaching Persian painters to work in European style, and his efforts in this direction were all too successful; among the most successful students was Isma'il Jalayir. The most prominent painters in the latter part of his reign were the poet Mahmud Khan and Muhammad Ghaffari, a nephew of Abu'l-Hasan, usually known by his title of Kamal al-Mulk; the former's landscapes and the latter's portraits, mostly executed in oils, are meticulously painted and almost photographic in effect.

The death of Nasir al-Din in 1896 – the end of the *ancien régime* – is a convenient stopping-place in this brief survey of Persian painting. The art is still extensively practised in Perisa, and art schools flourish in the chief cities. Some modern miniatures are of very high quality, but it is too early yet to see them in their correct perspective. Many are rather too dependent on the works of their predecessors, and at present there seems to be no artist of the stature of Bihzad, Sultan Muhammad, or even Riza-yi 'Abbasi. But the art has always had its ups and downs, and we may hope, perhaps, that an upward swing of the pendulum has begun.

5

Persian Architecture

D. N. WILBER

It has been frequently, and soundly, remarked that the history of Iranian culture exhibits a remarkable persistency and continuity of themes and methods of expression. This is notably the case throughout Iranian art and architecture. Over many centuries the emphasis was on decorative and, usually, non-representational forms: forms that were most often based on geometric or floral patterns. In architecture these forms became colourful and elaborate, but were always put forward as recognizable units which accentuated the major surfaces of the structures. The decoration enhanced the basic features of the buildings, rather than competed with them.

The builders of Iran, like those of the Western world, experimented with materials and methods of construction so that there was steady stylistic development. This development moved forward more slowly in Iran and other Moslem countries than in the West, as for example in mediaeval times in the development from Romanesque to Gothic styles. Experimentation with architectural forms merely for the sake of the novel and the new was not favoured. When an adequate solution to an architectural problem had been found, such as how to set a round dome on a square chamber, there was no real urge to seek additional solutions. Instead, there was a much stronger interest in exploring all the inherent decorative possibilities of several materials – of stone, of brick, of plaster, and of faience. Decoration was also stressed because there were only a few types of structures in use, and these had rather standardized plans. Climate also played a role in bringing in the use of very brilliant colours in architectural decoration: such a strong sun shone for most of the year that its rays would have bleached away – to the eyes of the observer – less bold colours.

Most Iranian architecture was essentially interior architecture. A building was not intended to be admired from a distance or to be walked around. Although a mosque, for example, might offer one towering entrance façade the rest of its exterior walls were surrounded by other buildings. The façade existed primarily as a passage to the interior court or courts. Such was the case at Persepolis and, hundreds of years later, at the shrine of the Imam Riza at Mashhad.

A relatively few different kinds of buildings were in common use. There were palaces; religious structures; including mosques, *madrasehs* (religious schools), shrines, tombs and temples, caravanserais; bridges; and baths. Prior to the advent of Islam, stone was favoured over brick as a building material. Then, it gave way, except for foundations and special uses, to brick. The bricks were either oven baked or sun-dried. Most of the structures that have survived are of baked brick, those of sun-dried brick were very susceptible to destruction from rain and snow. And yet, there probably were ten structures built of sun-dried brick to every one made of baked brick.

Palaces have survived from the Achaemenid and Sasanian periods, but from the Islamic period there are only fragmentary sections of such structures uncovered in archaeological excavations. The palaces erected for these rulers were often hastily thrown up of sun-dried brick and the walls were then covered with white plaster. Also, a ruler was strongly disinclined to living in a palace erected by a predecessor; he built a new one for himself and the earlier ones were deserted and crumbled into ruin.

Symbolism played no important role in Iranian architecture. During the Islamic centuries the dome was the most important architectural feature. Used over the principal chamber of the mosque and above the central area of a monumental tomb, it did take on a symbolic religious significance. For this reason, the domes became large in diameter and rose higher and higher into the air. Many of these domes were clad in blue faience, and blue also became associated with religious structures. Blue or gilded, gilded as at Qum and Mashhad, these soaring domes sparkle in the sun to be seen by the traveller long before the town itself comes into view.

In Iran monumental architecture appeared with the founding of the Achaemenid empire. Two features characterize early monumental architecture at whatever time and region it appears. First, elements of the structures are of permanent materials, which replace forms done before in less permanent ones: usually, as in Iran, stone replaced wood. Second, these structures are built carefully and deliberately to last a very long time, even, according to some of their inscriptions, 'for ever'.

On the main highway and some forty miles north of Persepolis is Pasargadae, the first capital of the Achaemenid empire. Within a defensive wall a number of palace pavilions flanked a central avenue. Of these excavated structures, only floor slabs, fragments of reliefs, and column bases and column drums remain. Nearby is the much better preserved tomb of Cyrus the Great. Constructed entirely of limestone, it is a direct copy, made larger, of a wooden house with a gable roof, and it is set on a base formed by six rows of stone steps. Nearly two centuries later Alexander the Great, in his triumphal campaign across Asia, visited the tomb: he found it had been robbed and he resealed its door with his own signet ring. Pasargadae marked the settlement of the rulers of a nomadic people by its permanent, monumental structures, while Persepolis was a magnificent reflection of the first great world empire. Founded by Darius the Great, and continued by his successors, the site was surpassed in military and commercial importance by Susa (Shush) and Hamadan (Ecbatana). It was, however, the spiritual heart of the empire to which tributes and gifts from all of the provinces of the empire were brought on the occasion of the New Year (21st March – the spring equinox).

Persepolis occupies a lofty terrace overlooking a fertile valley; the terrace was created in part by levelling rocky outcroppings, and in part, by filling in lower areas. The terrace area was encircled by high walls: visitors to the site enjoy the view over the valley without realizing that the original walls cut off all such views. From the plain a double-flight stairway, with each step or stair sufficiently shallow to be mounted by a horseman led to the terrace. Distinguished visitors and guests then moved through a portal of 'All-lands', and then entered a series of narrow courts which gave access to audience halls and palaces. These structures included two audience halls, the *apadana* and the so-called 'hall of a hundred columns'. The stairways leading to the *apadana* are covered with scenes, carved in low relief on slabs of stone, of the peoples from every corner of the vast empire moving through lines of

Persian and Median guards and bringing offerings from their homes – animals, precious metals and objects of fine craftsmanship. Other structures on the terrace included the treasury, and the private palaces of Darius and Xerxes.

Persepolis was burned by Alexander the Great, presumably in revenge for the earlier firing of Athens by the Persians. Centuries elapsed before efforts were made to uncover the ruins: now the excavations have so far advanced that detailed plans of all the structures have been made. Indeed, material is at hand to reconstruct and to restore Persepolis as it was at the height of the Achaemenid empire.

At Susa excavations have been continued for scores of years: the finds include a palace complex begun by Darius and a statue of this ruler. At Hamadan the Achaemenid site is deeply buried beneath the modern town, but from time to time gold cups and plaques of gold are recovered in casual digging. The architecture of the Achaemenid period was a very eclectic style which reflected influences from every corner of the ancient world. Workmen and materials were brought from Egypt, India, Asia Minor, and other provinces of the empire and their special techniques were clearly reflected in the details of the decoration of the architecture at Persepolis. Evidence for the presence of these foreign workmen is abundant: recorded on the inscriptions carved on the monuments and on the great number of baked clay tablets which recorded the payments made to these same artisans.

Above Persepolis were to be found the rock cut tombs of Artaxerxes II and Artaxerxes III. Some distance across the plain from Persepolis lies a sheer cliff called Naqsh-i Rustam with its rock-cut tombs of Darius I, Darius II, Xerxes and Artaxerxes I. In front of the tomb of Artaxerxes is a fire temple of the Achaemenid period – the so-called Ka'beh-yi Zardusht, a structure of dressed stone in several levels.

As is well known, the Achaemenid empire was destroyed by Alexander, who himself died before his thirty-third birthday and before he was able to consolidate his far-flung holdings. A branch of his successors to power, the Seleucids, made no real impact on the architecture of the region. It was not until the time of the Parthians, also known to history as the Arsacids, that a fresh vitality was found in architecture. Most of the Parthian palaces were erected to the west of the Iranian plateau proper: they included palaces and houses, religious structures and tombs – all built of baked bricks and stone. Of special note was the *ivan*, the element which was to become a major feature of the architecture of Islamic Iran – a long, rectangular tunnel-vaulted hall with an open façade and three sides flanked by walls. These *ivans* bridged the change from the post-and-lintel building of pre-Achaemenid times to the vaulted construction of all succeeding periods.

In the Sasanian period a line of rulers with great pride in their lineage and their homeland also proved to be great patrons of architecture. Palaces and fire temples were the principal monumental products, but city planning was not neglected – a circular plan with radiating streets was favoured. Stone masonry was the favoured material, followed by baked brick, while exterior and interior surfaces were coated with plaster: the plaster was painted or carved with relief patterns.

Five great palace complexes have survived in from fair to poor condition: at Firuzabad, Shapur, and Sarvistan in Fars province; at Qasr-i Shirin in western Iran; and at Ctesiphon on the lower Tigris River in Iraq. Quite characteristic of the plans and construction features of these palaces is that at Firuzabad, built in the 3rd century AD. The structure is a rectangle nearly 200 feet wide and 340 feet in depth: in the centre of the façade a great *ivan* opens into a square-domed throne chamber, and at the back of this area, living rooms are arranged around an interior court. All the rooms were crowned either by domes or by vaults. The palace at Ctesiphon featured a great vaulted *ivan*, now almost entirely in ruins, which rose to a height of 90 feet, was 75 feet wide, and was about 150 feet deep: these dimensions are given only to suggest its size – large enough to swallow up a small cathedral.

Mazdaism, the state religion of Sasanian times, was celebrated in fire temples throughout the land. Several major temples have been excavated, while more than a score of others have survived. Many of these temples stand on imposing heights so that their burning fires would have been visible for great distances; possibly the temples formed chains that stretched across the land with each fire visible from two others. Each such temple had, as its basic element, a square chamber crowned by a dome. Four wide arched portals led, one from each exterior side, to this chamber and they were probably never closed off in any way, so that the fire could be clearly seen. The dome over the square chamber was placed on four small arches that bridged the corners of the chamber; these arches were called squinches. While other lands and other cultures developed other ways of placing the dome on the square,

Iran always clung to the solution discovered at least as early as the 3rd century AD. The fundamental features of the mosques and other religious structures of Islamic Iran were established during the Sasanian period. These included the *ivan*; the major chamber, square in plan and crowned by a spacious dome; the interior court; and the use of vaulting over all the auxiliary rooms.

Following the Arab invasion of Iran and the rapid conversion of many of its people to Islam, there was an urgent need to establish mosques (*masjid*) in which the believers assembled for prayers. This was still so early in the history of Islam that the mosque plan was fluid; the only fixed elements were a large enclosed space and a *manar*, minaret, from which the faithful were called to prayer. As a result, many buildings in Iran were converted into mosques. When mosques and tombs were constructed, they reflected Sasanian prototypes. The tombs followed the plans and construction forms of the fire temples, while the mosques included elements common to the palaces.

It took a good many years for the local builders to arrive at what may be called the standard mosque plan. This plan has many variations, but its basic features are similar. An entrance *ivan* leads into a large open court, rectangular in shape and with a pool for ablutions at its centre. Each façade of the court displays arched arcades and at the centre of each side is an *ivan*: behind the arcades are prayer halls. On axis with the entrance and at the far side of the court is the sanctuary, a square chamber crowned by a dome. Into the wall of the sanctuary is set the *mihrab*, prayer niche, which is flanked by a *minbar*, pulpit. The *mihrab* indicates the direction of Mecca, toward which the prayers are offered, and it is in this direction that the entrance and the long axis of the mosque are oriented. There is at least one minaret, and possibly a number rising from either side of the *ivans*. Relatively few mosques were built to this standard plan at one time, many more arrived at it over a long period during which additions and changes were made to the first structure on the

ABOVE
Masjid-i Shaikh Lutfullah. Exterior portal façade
Collection of D. N. Wilber

BELOW
Masjid-i Shah. One of the court *ivans* and adjacent arcades
Collection of D. N. Wilber

site. The *madraseh*, religious school, employed this same standard plan: its arcades were frequently in two storeys, with rooms for students at both levels.

Within Iran hundreds of mosques of interest have survived and even more tombs and shrines are to be seen throughout the country so that it is impossible to offer more than a general account of these monuments. In addition to the major features identified in the introductory remarks, a few precise trends should be indicated. One, the fabric of the structures was lightened and attenuated. As the builders became familiar with the precise relationships between weights and supports the massive walls became thinner, openings wider and higher, and the vertical lines of the structures were given strong emphasis. Two, an amazing genius was displayed in the construction of domes and vaults. Domes became double. If a single dome had soared high above a chamber the space envelope would have been very tall and thin in relation to the plan of the chamber. Therefore, the builders put in a lower dome with proportions in harmony with the other dimensions of the chamber, leaving an empty area between the two domes. A great many types of vaults were built over square and rectangular areas. The architecture of medieval Europe was featured by splendid vaulting, but the brick vaults of Iran have as much artistic merit as the stone vaults of the Gothic period. Indeed, the vaults of Iran have a claim to greater engineering skill. Normally a vault is held up by a framework or scaffold of wood until the mortar joints between the stones or bricks have set; otherwise the vault would simply collapse. The Iranian builders, however, developed methods of erecting domes and vaults without using any supporting elements. These technical methods can scarcely be described here, but they reflect great ingenuity. Three, the Iranian style of Islamic architecture early became quite distinct from the styles of the monuments of India, Asia Minor (Turkey) and Egypt. In part, this distinctive character was the result of plan types and construction materials in use before the advent of Islam, but it was also the outcome of a special Iranian

ABOVE
Madraseh Madar-i Shah. Dome, sanctuary *ivan*
and minarets
Collection of D. N. Wilber

BELOW
Madraseh Madar-i Shah. Court arcades
Collection of D. N. Wilber

sensibility for form and colour. This sensibility was passed down in families of skilled craftsmen over many generations, with the details of design and construction probably recorded in pattern books that went with the builders on their travels.

Were we able to look at many monuments in each of the historical periods of the Islamic era we could trace both general and specific stylistic developments. The 'naked' brickwork of the Seljuq period would be seen to give way to the more sophisticated, lighter structures of the Il-Khanid (Mongol) period, with colour just beginning to play a conspicuous role. Then would come the stately Timurid monuments at Herat and Mashhad, clad in glorious faience mosaic in which blues stand out, and then the Safavid period, fortunately well represented throughout Iran by a variety of types of structures. A decline in taste and techniques did set in later in the Safavid period and the monuments of Qajar times bring aspects of this decline to the fore, while retaining a certain informal charm. Since, however, we are not able to look at a large number of monuments, let attention be concentrated on four of the greatest monuments, or complexes of structures, of Iran – sites that every visitor to the country should see.

In the 10th century AD, the southern shore of the Caspian Sea, a relatively isolated area that had not been converted to Islam until the 9th century, was the setting for the rise of the Ziyarid dynasty. Most notable of this line was Qabus ibn Vashmgir, a warrior and a man of letters, whose reign was interrupted by a period of exile and ended with his assassination. His tomb is one of the most striking monuments erected in any country in any period. Built of baked brick, it is a tapering cylinder, relieved by ten out-jutting triangular flanges, topped by a cone-shaped roof. The height from the ground to the top of the cone is 160 feet; the diameter is 56 feet and the walls are 17 feet thick. Circling the cylinder, near its top, is an Arabic inscription in the so-called Kufic script which reads: 'In the name of Allah, the merciful, the compassionate; this castle was built by the Amir Shams al-Ma'ali the Amir, son of the Amir, Qabus ibn Vashmgir, who ordered it built during his lifetime in the lunar year 397 and the solar year 375 (AD1007).' According to one early historian, the body of Qabus was in a glass coffin suspended in the interior from chains hanging from the dome. Since excavations below the floor of the structure revealed no traces of a burial, this account has some plausibility. Placed on a high artificial mound, the soaring shaft is visible for miles around and the shifting shadows cast by the flanges on the cylinder serve to enhance the vigour and boldness of the Gunbad-i Qabus.

The greatest structure of the Il-Khanid (Mongol) period is the tomb of Öljeitü, one of the rulers of this line, at Sultaniya. Even in its badly damaged state, it is one of the world's architectural masterpieces. Its construction was begun about 1305, along with a vast campaign of building at the site of this new capital of the realm. About 1309 Öljeitü transferred his allegiance from the Sunni sect to the Shi'a sect of Islam, and planned to transport the remains of the Shi'a martyrs from Iraq for reburial in this structure – hence attracting crowds of pilgrims. Soon, however, he reverted to Sunnism and much of the mausoleum was redecorated in order to conceal the surfaces on which the name of 'Ali, the Shi'a martyr, appeared.

The mausoleum is basically an octagon, with the north exterior squared off and a mortuary chapel attached on the south. The interior chamber, crowned by a great dome, is nearly 26 metres in diameter, and it is about 50 metres from the floor level to the inner surface of the dome. A lofty gallery encircles the mausoleum, and eight minarets spring from the corner angles to ring the dome which was coated with light blue glazed bricks. Thousands of builders must have been assembled from all Iran for the building of Sultaniyeh and the mausoleum of Öljeitü. After the completion of the work they scattered to their home towns to put into practice the new skills, notably that of the use of colour – colour on plaster and colour in faience panels. Sultaniyeh was the capital of Iran for only a very few years, yet the monuments of its short life remain. And this same pattern of rulers choosing new sites for capitals was established and continued in later centuries; it is to this habit of changing capitals – as rulers changed palaces – that Iran has had so many monuments preserved in so many centres.

The largest and most sacred shrine of Iran and its principal place of pilgrimage is that of the Imam Riza at Mashhad. 'Ali Riza, the eighth imam of the Shi'a sect, died of poison early in the 9th century. In subsequent times more and more architectural elements grew up around this tomb and the town took the name of Mashhad, or 'burial place of a martyr'. Today a wide circular avenue encompasses the shrine which comprises numerous courts and structures of many periods. The finest of these is the Masjid-i Gauhar Shad – the mosque built by the order of the wife of Shah Rukh, son of Timur. The architect was Qavam al-Din Shirazi and the work was completed about 1418 according to an inscription designed by a son of the queen. The faience mosaic inscription of white letters on a dark blue ground states that Gauhar Shad built the mosque with her private funds, and her son calls his mother, 'Her Highness, the Noble in Greatness, the Sun of the Heaven of Chastity and Continence, Famous for Nobility and Honour and Piety. . . .' Since the mosque was literally embedded in earlier structures, it has no exterior walls. The plan displays four *ivans* facing the open court, with prayer halls filling in the area behind the arcades. An enormously high and deep *ivan* comprises the entire sanctuary area. Minarets flanking the façade of the *ivan* spring from the ground level, rather than from the top of its façade as in earlier examples. The dome above the sanctuary is slightly bulbous in profile: as large as it is, it is not the major feature of the structure for it is masked by the high façade of the *ivan*. The major interest of the mosque is the splendid faience mosaic which flows over every square inch of the structure: in design, in skilled execution, and in brilliant harmonious colours this faience was never surpassed. Geometric patterns prevail on the surfaces of the piers, minarets and wall panels; floral arabesques coil over the spandrels; and stately inscriptions frame the *ivans* and march in horizontal rows along the court arcades. Only the sanctuary chamber was not clad in faience: the architect was experimenting with a new technique for the walls are covered with white plaster and the zone of transition below the dome is a cloud of plaster stalactites – row on row of honeycomb forms.

Isfahan is a living memorial to Shah 'Abbas, greatest ruler of the Safavid line. In 1598 he ordered construction begun on an imperial city; the site was a region of orchards and fields between the Zayandeh-Rud and the very old town of Isfahan. In the first stage the general plan was established and construction begun, while in the second stage, after 1611, the major structures were erected. The over-all plan was as follows. From the south a wide promenade avenue crossed the Zayandeh-Rud and ran north, bordered by gardens, and adorned with palaces and pavilions. This avenue, the Chahar Bagh, or Four Gardens, ended abruptly where a portal on the east side gave access to the royal living quarters – an area of palaces, gardens, pavilions, workshops, storehouses and stables. To the east of this area lay the Maidan-i Shah, the Imperial Square, a vast rectangle with its long axis running north to south. At its northern end was a monumental entrance to the older covered bazaars, and at the southern end the Masjid-i Shah. On the west the ʿAli Qapu, the Lofty Gate, provided a ceremonial entrance to the royal area, while to the east stood the Masjid-i Shaikh Lutfullah.

The earliest structure to rise along the Maidan-i Shah was the Masjid-i Shaikh Lutfullah, built between 1603 and 1609. Its plan is the essence of simplicity; a square chamber crowned by a dome. The portal, recessed from the line of two storey arcades which front the square has splendid faience mosaic. The slightly pointed dome rises in an unbroken contour from a circular drum: swirling floral arabesques on a warm buff-coloured ground are done in faience mosaic. The interior is a lovely jewel box, every area is clad in glowing tile work; blue predominates at the lower levels, while the dome culminates in a sunburst of golden yellow.

The monumental entrance to the bazaar, at the northern end of the square, was completed in 1617. In 1619 the rear wall of this lofty portal was decorated with a huge painting portraying Shah ʿAbbas victorious in battle over the Özbegs. At the southern end, construction began on the Masjid-i Shah in 1611 and continued until 1637. As the plan was established, an adjustment had to be made to compensate for the difference between the north–south axis of the square, and the *qibleh* axis of the mosque – the direction of Mecca. As a result one sees the great entrance portal with its flanking minarets as one unit, while some distance to the right the great dome and its *ivan* portal loom high above the court arcades. The plan of the Masjid-i Shah, the standard four *ivan* type with some added elements, is reminiscent of that of the Masjid-i Gauhar Shad at Mashhad. In contrast, however, the longer dimensions of the large open court is at right angles to the main axis, rather than parallel to it as at Mashhad. The major unit of the mosque, on the south of the court, includes an *ivan*, the square dome chamber, and flanking oratories. The surfaces are covered with either faience mosaic or *haft rangi* tiles. In faience mosaic, well developed in the Timurid period, a full scale pattern was prepared on the ground. Then thousands of tiny pieces, chipped from solid colour tiles, were laid face down on the pattern. Plaster was used to coat the back and after it hardened the panel was set into position on the structure. Later this costly, time-consuming process tended to give way to *haft rangi* 'seven colours', in which a segment of the pattern was drawn on each of a number of square tiles, as many as seven earth pigments were applied to the tiles, and then they were fired in a kiln.

Today the Masjid-i Shah appears as fresh and shining as at the moment of its completion, thanks to long years spent in reinforcing its inadequate foundations and in replacing missing sections of the faience decoration.

The date of the construction of the ʿAli Qapu, on the west side of the square, is not known; it may have been shortly after 1598. The first skyscraper in Iran, it rises six storeys, and served the multiple functions of a monumental entrance to the royal area, an administrative centre, a place of reception for foreign embassies, and a point of vista over the great square. On the fourth floor a porch with eighteen tall wooden columns overlooks the *maidan*, and from this porch Shah ʿAbbas watched polo games and archery contests. The many rooms, all small, still retain colourful paintings of birds and animals in flowering trees and shrubs, as well as panels portraying men and women in scenes of courtly pleasure in gardens – the costumes of these figures reflect the influence of European painters who worked at the court.

From the central archway of the ʿAli Qapu, a corridor led west into the palace grounds. Most of the pavilions and palaces that stood in these grounds have long since vanished. A noble exception is the Chihil Sutun ('forty pillars') garden palace, erected about 1620. Rectangular in plan, its most striking feature is a spacious open porch whose wooden roof is supported on eighteen towering wood columns. The porch fronts on a very long reflecting pool, and is provided with its own pool – a great marble basin. The open recess back of the porch is sheathed in mirrors, and the recess gives access to a banqueting hall that extends the full width of the structure.

At the dado level are paintings depicting rustic pleasures similar to those in the ʿAli Qapu, while on the upper walls are six huge oil paintings.

The Chahar Bagh promenade was carried across the river on a stately bridge, decorated with faience mosaic and built by a general of Shah ʿAbbas. Between 1706 and 1714 and during the reign of Shah Sultan Husain, the so-called Madraseh Madar-i Shah (School of the Mother of the Shah) was erected along the Chahar Bagh. The plan displays four *ivans*, and a great dome rises above the sanctuary chamber. In its scale and in its splendid decoration, this dome rivals that of the Masjid-i Shah, erected nearly a century earlier.

Important monuments of the Safavid period are to be found at towns and shrines throughout Iran, and it was this period which saw the final, majestic manifestation of Persian architecture. In the 18th century there was a revival of building centred at Shiraz in which a sense of gaiety and informality was stressed; while during the Qajar dynasty, which reigned from Tehran from the end of the 18th century until 1925, foreign influences, notably from Russia, permeated the royal palaces and even certain features of the religious structures.

Under the reigning Pahlavi dynasty certain architects choose to follow the so-called 'international style', while others employ the decorative details and materials of earlier centuries in their designs. Whether by means of this conscious attempt to relate to the past, or because the architectural monuments are carefully preserved and protected, it is certain that this great national heritage will long endure.

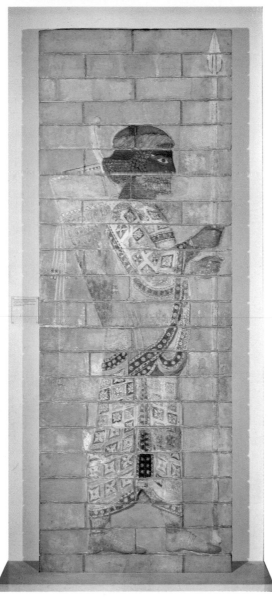

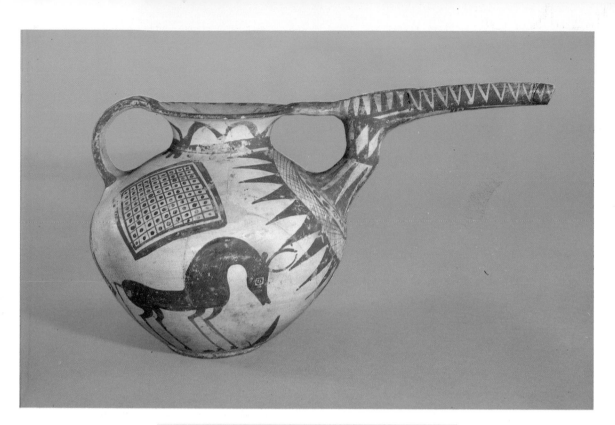

6

᪥᪥

Persian Pottery

R. H. PINDER-WILSON

From very early times men have fashioned vessels for cooking, eating and storage from clay, rendering it hard by firing. The potter's art arose when men were no longer content to be limited by the exclusively practical nature of their vessels and began to use them as a means of expressing artistic ideas.

In Iran the potter's art has been practised almost continuously since at least 6000BC. Although many details still await clarification, the main lines of its development are now drawn, thanks to the labours of the archaeologist and art historian over the last hundred years. A detailed history of Iranian pottery is not within the present scope; and only its principal characteristics and achievements can be attempted.

While the tradition of pottery-making in Iran is a continuous one, there are two periods which have found their finest and most characteristic expression in pottery: the three millennia covering the Chalcolithic period and the thousand years subsequent to Iran's entry into the Islamic world.

The earliest pottery in Iran has been found at Tepe Sarab near Kermanshah and dates from about 6000BC. Even at this early date the Iranian potter was proving

ABOVE
Spouted Jar. Pottery, painted in red. Early
1st millennium BC
British Museum 129072
By courtesy of the Trustees of the British Museum

BELOW
Base of Qaliyan (tobacco-pipe). Pottery, painted
in underglaze black and blue, *c* AD 1600
British Museum OA 1910 5–11 2
By courtesy of the Trustees of the British Museum

his skill as a modeller of clay for the Tepe Sarab finds include two remarkable pottery figurines, the one a seated female figure and the other a boar. In the Neolithic period, painted pottery was being made alongside the more utilitarian wares; but it was in the Chalcolithic period that the great painted wares were being produced at sites on the plateau and in the valleys of the Zagros mountains. These beautiful vessels are painted with black designs on a red or buff ground. At Tepe Sialk near Kashan their development can be followed as the result of the excavation of successive occupation levels: the earlier combination of geometric and abstract designs is replaced by representation of the ibex and finally the introduction of naturalistically rendered birds and animals. There were also important technological changes: finer body material, improved firing methods which produced a buff or cream ground instead of red and above all the introduction of the potter's wheel sometime in the second half of the fourth millennium BC, which made possible a greater degree of control and of execution. The finest of these wares were made in Susa in the lowland region of south-western Iran. The famous beaker now in the Louvre decorated with panels each containing an ibex with great sweeping horns and a frieze of Saluki hounds is a masterpiece of linear design appropriate to the shape of the vessel.

Many technical and artistic innovations were made in Iran during the Bronze and Iron Ages. Notable are the vessels in the form of bulls, stags and other creatures made in the south-western Caspian region; and a characteristic long spouted jar with painted decoration from Sialk and dating from the end of the second millennium and beginning of the first millennium BC. An important technical advance was the introduction of glazed earthenware and faience into Elam where remarkable glazed tiles have been found at Choga Zambil. Subsequently, glazed earthenware was made in western and north-western Iran; and the perfected technique can be seen in the famous panels of polychrome glazed tiles from the Achaemenid palaces at Susa. A blue or green alkaline glaze continued to be applied to pottery vessels during the Parthian and Sasanian periods.

These advances contributed to the flowering of Iran's second great period of pottery production. In AD762 the city of Baghdad was founded as the capital of the 'Abbasid Caliphate and Iran now played a dominant role in the administrative and cultural life of the empire. The requirements of the Caliph's court and great officers of state stimulated the development of the industrial arts; and although the earliest distinctively Islamic pottery was produced in Iraq, it would be surprising if there were not Iranian potters among those working for the Caliph and his circle, since that country had for long been under Iranian rule.

The pottery of Iraq in the 'Abbasid period represents the development of ancient techniques as well as the discovery of new ones. Among the former was the use of the opaque white tin glaze now revived in order to simulate the surface of the white porcelains imported at this time from China. Among the latter was the technique of lustre painting on pottery. It is possible that tin-glazed wares with painting in cobalt and green were manufactured in Iran and it is certain that the so-called splashed ware – in imitation of the contemporary T'ang ware of China – was made at centres in Iran besides those of Iraq.

Incontestible is the contribution of the potters of Khurasan in the 9th to 11th centuries AD. They painted their vessels in coloured clay slips which they then covered with a transparent lead glaze. The process was wholly original and their vessels – mostly bowls – some painted in brilliant but harmonious colours with fantastic flowers or geometric patterns and others with Arabic inscriptions in monumental Kufic characters in red or black on a white ground, are masterpieces of Iranian pottery.

The establishment of the Turkish dynasty of the Seljuqs in the 11th century brought about a re-orientation of Islamic art in which Iran played a decisive part. In many respects the pottery of the 12th and 13th centuries represents the highest achievement of the Iranian potter by virtue of three important technical innovations. First, the discovery of a fine, hard and thin body material made it possible to produce vessels which could really match the quality of potting found in the Sung porcelains of China: secondly, this new type of body, with which the alkaline glaze satisfactorily fused, was combined with true underglaze painting – a far more fluent medium than the coloured clay slip. Lastly the discovery of overglaze enamels enlarged the palette of the potter – the so-called *mina'i* ware executed both in underglaze colours and overglaze enamels has a range of seven colours. These wares are decorated with floral and arabesque scrolls, birds and animals and geometric designs presented in characteristic Seljuq style as well as pictorial representations of elaborate scenes – in rare cases narrative. Similar schemes of decoration occur in the lustre painted wares which were being produced at Ray, Kashan and perhaps other centres in this period. Less spectacular but quite as appealing are the monochrome wares – white, turquoise or cobalt blue with carved or moulded decoration under the glaze.

In the Timurid period the production of fine wares appears to have declined, perhaps on account of the increased importation of porcelain from China. A few examples of Timurid pottery include imitations of Chinese blue and white decorated porcelain and celadons. The Timurid contribution was rather the development of glazed tilework which had already been revived in the Seljuq period: and it was in the 15th century that the finest mosaic tile revetments were made.

A revival of the pottery industry was inaugurated under the patronage of Shah 'Abbas the Great. The best wares of the Safavid period can stand comparison with those of the Seljuq period. As in previous periods, a principal source of inspiration was Chinese porcelain: and the Safavid blue and white decorated ware in which 'Chinoiserie' themes were skilfully adapted to the Iranian decorative style are often as beautiful as their Chinese originals. Lustre painting on pottery was also revived and the finest examples decorated in the current Safavid style are worthy successors of the products of Ray and Kashan. The most notable achievement of the ceramic art in the Safavid period was tilework, both mosaic tile and the newly introduced 'cuerda seca' technique which allowed greater manipulation of drawing. It is the tilework that adds so much to the allure of the great Safavid monuments of Isfahan and other cities of Iran.

Panels of coloured tiles were employed both on the exterior and interior of buildings. In this way colour was introduced into what would otherwise be a monotonous surface of plain brick. Such panels were also intended to give added emphasis to the architectonic elements. In the same way, the Persian potter has always proved himself adept in enhancing the form of his vessel by his choice of surface decoration.

ABOVE
Bowl. Pottery, painted in slip under colourless glaze. Nishapur, 9th century AD
British Museum OA 1967 12–13 1
By courtesy of the Trustees of the British Museum

BELOW
Bowl. Pottery, painted in underglaze colours and enamels. Early 13th century AD
British Museum OA 1912 12–7 3
By courtesy of the Trustees of the British Museum

7

Persian Carpets

G. WILFRID SEAGER

The discovery of a Persian carpet in the village of Pazyryk in the Altai mountains, in southern Siberia, shows that the art of pile-carpet weaving is probably as old as the Persian monarchy, for the Pazyryk treasures are said to date from the 5th century BC. From the fineness of weave of this carpet – it contains some 184 knots to the square inch – and the high standard of its design, one may safely assume that the art had been practised for some considerable period previously.

The discovery of a pile carpet of about 2,500 years of age is of importance for another reason also. The word 'carpet' has been used to describe fabrics seen and reported by historians and early travellers. Without the positive evidence of a piece of the material, it has been suspected that the exquisitely designed fabrics described may have been of flat tapestry weave. There can therefore now be no doubt that the art of weaving pile fabrics is older even than the Pazyryk rug, which is now in the Hermitage Museum, Leningrad, in a carefully sealed case, protected against the risk of damage from climatic changes. The degree of skill shown in its construction and the closely executed symmetry of its balanced design, with a well-covered

The Pazyryk carpet, 5th century BC
The Hermitage Museum, Leningrad

field framed in a wide border with narrow guards on either side, show conclusively that the weaver was no novice.

It is exciting to have this proof that Persian pile-carpet weaving is at least two and a half millennia old and also to learn from this carpet that thus early the convention of ground, border and guards, which has been observed ever since, had already been established. The design shows that the use of human and animal forms, pictured naturally, was already being utilized in a decorative way. This is a technique in which the Persian artistic genius excels and it reached its zenith in the 15th, 16th and early 17th centuries when weavers delighted to reproduce copies of hunting scenes or stories from the *Shahnameh* as depicted in miniatures of the period.

It is a human failing, from one generation to the next, to decry contemporary art by comparison with the allegedly superior achievements of preceding generations. A 17th century traveller reported that the products of Isfahan looms had in some cases sunk so low that they were allowed to rot into compost to enrich the soil of the gardens outside the city. In 1892 Lord Curzon wrote of the deterioration of the Persian weavers' craft because of their use of western synthetic dyes, at that time fast neither to light nor water. In his opinion Persian carpets were never again to attain their former excellence. 'Never' is an awfully long time! One wonders whether travellers in the days of Shah 'Abbas wrote in similarly scornful terms of contemporary carpets when compared with Timurid carpets of a century earlier.

The truth is that the spread of culture westwards created a taste for their products which Persian weavers struggled to satisfy. Persian carpet output had to grow to meet this increasing demand. Whereas formerly those who could afford to carpet their homes with hand-knotted floor-coverings were few in number, gradually more and more Persian carpets were sought after, for instead of the possession of carpets being confined to princely families, the nobility, or wealthy land-owners, upon whose patronage weavers depended, weavers soon found themselves compelled to produce a much wider range of qualities so that their carpets might reach a wider public of equal discernment but of more slender means.

This growth in carpet production did not imply that carpets could no longer be made as fine in closeness of knots as those made for patrons who had no need to count the cost of production. Carpets as fine as ever could still be made. There are today a greater number of skilled craftsmen engaged in carpet weaving than ever before. Among so many, a few are technically more outstanding than their fellows. If a particular example must be quoted of recent exceptional craftsmanship, one may call attention to the carpets which came from the looms of Emogli of Mashhad some thirty years ago. The superlative carpets woven by his *ustads* – master craftsmen indeed – in arabesque designs reminiscent of the finest carpets shown in Timurid miniatures, achieved wide fame. Many found their way into royal palaces in Tehran. Some may be seen in reception rooms in the Majlis and the officers' club.

Carpet lovers will not agree unanimously as to which is the most beautiful Persian carpet. Fortunately, there are magnificent reproductions of the best-known historical carpets in such publications as the Vienna Museum folios of 1892 and 1908; Dr F. R. Martin's *History of Oriental Carpets Before 1800*, Vienna 1908; and, following the great Exhibition of Persian Art in London in 1931, Upham Pope's *Survey of Persian Art*, Oxford University Press, 1938.

Those who have made the closest study do agree, however, that the choice must lie within half a dozen or so. There are those who would choose such a carpet as Denmark's coronation carpet, on which Danish kings are crowned. This carpet, occasionally shown to visitors to the Rosenborg Palace in Copenhagen, consists of an all-over design on a gold ground and border. The best known carpet, as it is also the most frequently copied, is that in the Victoria and Albert Museum in London, made in 1539 by Maqsud Kashani for the shrine at Ardabil. Some experts prefer the hunting carpet in the Vienna Museum of Art and Industry; with 800 knots to the square inch it is perhaps the most closely-woven carpet left to us from the Safavid period. Yet, when we look at the incredible fineness of detail of that carpet, we should remind ourselves that the splendour of the Ardabil carpet was achieved with but 320 knots to the square inch, a miracle of perfection.

The magnificently woven carpet in the Berlin Kaiser Friedrich Museum, with its great medallion crowded with finely-drawn cranes in flight among scores of Chinese cloud motifs, was Dr Martin's choice in 1908. Wilhelm von Bode was then Director of the Berlin Museum. To Dr Martin's shocked surprise von Bode did not choose the carpet under his own care but named the most beautiful carpet to be the so-called 'Chelsea' carpet. This hangs on a wall at right angles to the Ardabil carpet which has pride of place in the Victoria and Albert Museum. Both the Berlin medallion carpet and the Chelsea carpet (so called because it was bought in a shop in the King's Road, Chelsea) are said to have been woven in about AD1450. This would make both of them a hundred years older than the Ardabil carpet.

Closeness of knotting alone is no criterion of beauty. The less closely-woven bolder Heriz carpets from the Bakshaish weaving district in Azarbaijan, with their masculine severity and assertive designs on brick-red grounds and their 'turtle' or 'samovar' patterned borders, have an attraction all their own. They are in a different class altogether from the classic picture carpets. The latter drew their inspiration from the Timurid and Safavid miniaturists of the Herat, Tabriz and Shiraz schools of artists who delighted to illustrate hunting scenes or stories from the wealth of Persian mythology and from Firdausi's *Shahnameh* tales of the kings. Miniaturists and carpet-designers both drew also upon the lyric poets for their subjects. One can at once visualize the miniature or carpet which might illustrate Sa'di's lines:

> '*O Cypress-tree with silver limbs,*
> *this colour and scent of thine*
> *Have shamed the scent of the myrtle-plant*
> *and the bloom of the eglantine.*
> *Judge with thine eyes, and set thy foot*
> *in the garden fair and free,*
> *And tread the jasmine under thy foot,*
> *and the flowers of the judas-tree.*'

One cannot accurately name the artists who created the designs of particular carpets woven 400 or 500 years ago, but the meticulous detail of the carpets illustrated in their pictures surely proves that these miniaturists were familiar with the conventions of carpet designing. Illustrations of carpets appeared profusely in palaces, royal tents and in garden scenes in these miniatures. Surely one may assume that these same artists themselves drew or at least supervised the preparation of loom-drawings for the finest carpets ever made. It would indeed be strange if this were not so.

The design of the border of the Chelsea carpet, with its distinctive interlocking crenellations, had already been used to decorate the inner frame of a table of contents of an anthology written for Baisunghur in Shiraz in 1420. This same design appeared again sixty years later, illustrating a manuscript of the *Khamseh* of Jami, the drawings of which were attributed to Qasim ʿAli and Maqsud, both pupils of Bihzad himself, perhaps the greatest miniaturist of them all. Is it being too imaginative to suggest that this Maqsud was the Maqsud Kashani of the Ardabil inscription, the slave of the shrine as he claimed? Surely it was not the weaver but the artist who designed the carpet.

Naturally enough, historians and travellers describe in detail only the finest examples of carpets seen by them on their travels. They make no mention of the more modest products of Persian carpet looms. Much though one admires the finest specimens yet there is great charm in the cruder, elementary designs and colours of some coarsely-woven tribal or village rug with, or even because of, its human diversities and faults. The more highly-skilled weavers would probably move with the Court from one place to another to make fine carpets for royal palaces or as princely gifts for foreign emissaries. The so-called 'Polish' carpets in gold and silver tapestry background, with wool or silk pile for the design, were made for such purposes. In a more modest way, however, weaving was carried on in the private homes of the people, each district, tribe or village developing its own particular style of weave.

It is more difficult to differentiate between the finest weaves, particularly in the case of carpets made several hundred years ago if, as one may suppose, they were made for patrons who required special designs and colours not necessarily associated with one place or another. Weavers in the tribes and villages did not travel outside their own areas as distances between places of production were great and travel, until recent times, was difficult. Therefore the peculiarities of each weaving district remained recognizably its own and justified Sir George Birdwood's expressing this in 1892, however pompously, in his monograph entitled *The Termless Antiquity, Historical Continuity and Integral Identity of the Oriental Manufacture of Sumptuary Carpets.* This 'integral identity' still exists, but improved communications have resulted in an exchange of designs, colourings and skills between neighbouring or even more distant areas. In this way the identification of one rug from another is becoming more difficult.

Certain means of identification may be noted. Weavers use either the Persian or the Turkish knot depending upon the practice of each area. This may be expressed geographically by drawing a line southwards from the Caspian through (or a little west of) Resht, Qazvin, Arak, Isfahan and Abadeh, down to the Province of Fars and the lands which separate the Qashqai weavers (who use the Turkish knot) from the Khamseh tribes (who use the Persian knot). All carpets woven west of this arbitrary line are made with the Turkish knot. East of the line all carpets – whether Persian, Indian or Chinese – are made with the Persian knot. Recognition of the knot is more easily learned from text-book diagrams (see below). The pile tips of the Turkish knot spring from within the loop at the base of the knot. The pile tips of the Persian knot come forward from each side of one of the two warp strands on which the knot is tied.

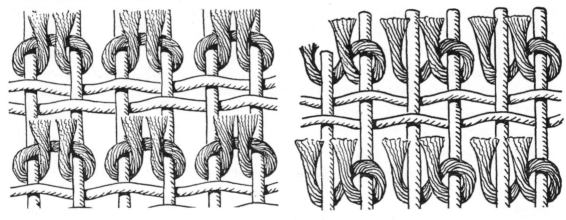

Turkish Knot   *Persian Knot*

There are exceptions to this arbitrary geographic line. Several places in Turkey have recently adopted the Persian knot as they find it less wasteful in yarn consumption. Some Turcoman Bokhara carpets show both knots in the same piece. Perhaps the most notable exception to the rule is provided by the Afshari weavers in Kirman province. Although their homes now lie east of the line, they weave with the Turkish knot because their original home was in Azarbaijan whence they were exiled to the south as punishment for their insurrection under Shah Tahmasp. Minor exceptions to this rule are due to the practice of weavers who live close to the line on either side or to intermarriage and the introduction on a small scale of one knot or the other within family units.

The three categories of weavers – tribal, village, or town – each have differing characteristics. Tribal looms are light and horizontal, being pegged out on the ground so that they may be easily collapsed and rolled up to be carried to the next grazing-ground, as the tribe migrates in spring and autumn. When the loom is pegged out, the working area is lifted free of the ground by a tripod support.

Understandably, the tribal rugs are the least developed. Theirs have the simplest designs, the most rudimentary and the fewest colours. Their designs take angular forms because the comparatively loose weave, due to fewer knots to the square inch and the coarser materials used, does not allow the weaver to knot closely-detailed patterns. Tribal rugs are woven in designs to which the weavers of each tribe, and sometimes each group of families within the tribe, have been accustomed for generations, being woven from memory without the help of loom-drawings. This accounts for the frequent oddities of pattern, where a forgetful weaver or his *shagird* (apprentice) has allowed his attention to stray and his fingers have knotted in some charming departure from the true repeat of the pattern in the corresponding di-agonally opposite quarter of the rug.

Tribal rugs are usually, or perhaps one should say were usually made of wool throughout – warp, weft and pile-knots – the wool off their sheep being the material most readily available and with the additional advantage that it transported itself on the march. Thus a tribal rug could easily be recognized from its long woollen fringes. In recent years many tribal families have settled in villages and these now sedentary weavers use cotton for their warps in place of wool. This makes for a straighter, firmer fabric but some of the former charm is lost and with it the wide decorative flat tapestry or *kilim* finish at either or both ends of the rug.

Apart from the primitive rugs made in the remoter parts of Fars, perhaps the simplest types of Persian rugs are those made by the Beluch tribes of eastern Khorasan, down through Seistan and into the Province of Kirman where their presence was noted as long ago as the 10th century.

Prior to the much regretted introduction of aniline dyes about ninety years ago, the only dyes used were vegetable except for cochineal. Madder was used for reds and roses; weld and indigo for greens and blues; vine leaves, pomegranate rinds, walnut husks and oak bark for biscuit and tan shades, camel colours and different depths of brown. Unhappily the use of aniline dyes still persists, though to a lesser extent than the use of chrome dyes. The former fade to unattractive shades, run into the next colour or, in an alkali solution, may disappear completely. When faded by exposure to light, the original colour is only discernible when the rug is turned over or the pile roots exposed.

Chrome dyes are undesirable for an exactly opposite reason. They are too fast and will not mellow as do the kinder vegetable dyes. Many rugs contain colours dyed by both methods. Here the mellowing will be uneven. Can we not have a return to vegetable dyes? Some twenty-five years or so ago a conference of experts in Tehran recommended just that. If that could not be; the conference suggested that the use of chrome dyes should be limited to the use of a feasible and simple dyeing technique which would more closely correspond to the effect of the use of vegetable dyes and would not be injurious to the enviable repute of Persian rugs. All true lovers of Persian carpets and rugs would welcome a return to the exclusive use of traditional vegetable dyeing methods.

Weavers in the villages and towns have vertical fixed looms, those in the towns being more perfectly made. The technique only varies on minor points such as the method of mounting the warp strands, passing the wefts, or finishing off the fringes and the sides. Some carpets and rugs have fringes at both ends, others at one end only because of the method of securing the warp strands at the start of weaving.

Village rugs are mostly woven from memory, but in some places such as Bijar in Kurdistan or in a few villages around Arak, a *vagireh* or sample prototype is hung in front of the loom for the weaver to copy and to repeat either over the whole ground or in the four quarters, as may be required by the design.

Tribal rugs are usually smaller than those produced in the villages for the reason that they may have to be carried unfinished from one place to another. The smallest are the Beluch rugs. These are oblong in shape compared with the Afshari rugs which are slightly larger and habitually more square. Qashqai and Khamseh tribal products are marketed in Shiraz and are made in a much wider assortment of sizes from mats up to small carpet sizes.

The Chelsea carpet, *c* AD 1450
Victoria and Albert Museum, Crown Copyright

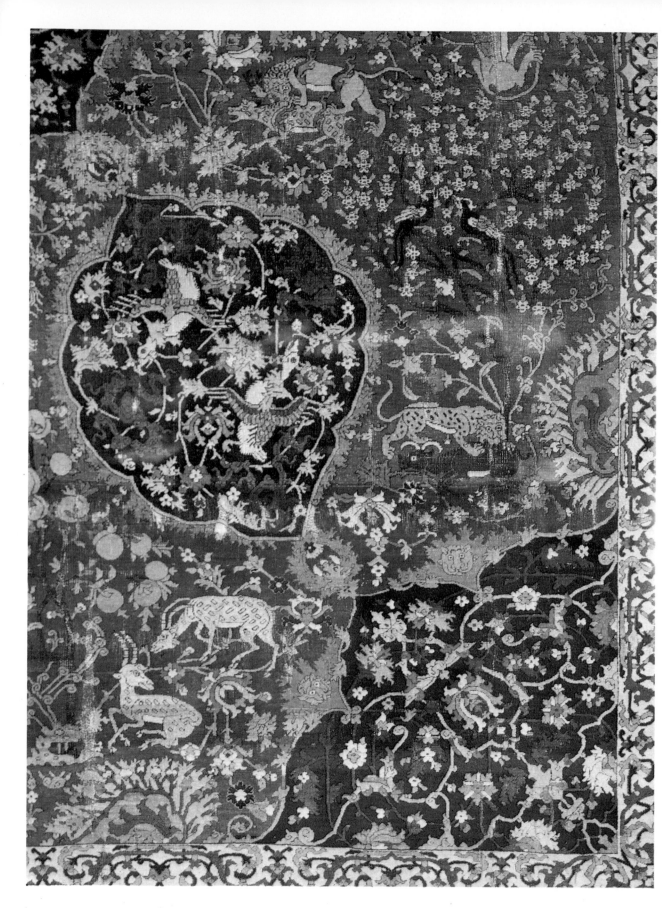

Although one includes Bakhtiari rugs in the nomadic category, they are not now made by those families which migrate twice yearly over the Zagros mountains, but in the villages of the Chahar Mahal south-west of Isfahan where weavers of Bakhtiari descent have now settled. They still use horizontal looms and sometimes weave very large carpets. Most are not large, however, varying from eight to ten feet long by about five to seven feet wide. They are of sturdy construction and strong in colour. The commonest design consists of a series of panels across the ground, each panel being occupied by some bold angular motif such as a cypress tree or a willow (Laila's legendary willow) with its branches weeping sometimes on one side and sometimes on the other or, less frequently, on both sides of the central trunk. Dark blues, dull red or orange, a generous use of bright or dull yellow and rather hard greens make a Bakhtiari carpet easily identifiable.

Although there are certain basic styles of design, each weaver interprets them differently. Very few village rugs are found to be exact pairs. Cecil Edwards, in *The Persian Carpet*, illustrated some 350 different carpets and rugs, typical of the various centres but by no means inclusive. Yet sixty years earlier Edward Stebbing in his monograph on the Ardabil carpet in 1892, wrote: 'There are now some twenty or more of the finest designs of the old carpets being produced with skill and fidelity . . . in place of the four or five designs to which the industry was (formerly) confined!' What did he mean?

Some motifs, in simple or elaborate form, may be found in use throughout Persia. The simplest and the most widely used is the pine-cone pattern which may be seen in row after row across the Saraband carpets and rugs of Arak, usually on a red ground but sometimes on cream or dark blue. In its most complicated form one may trace it in some elaborately entwined graceful design drawn by a Kirman artist. The pattern was more commonly used in the fine embroidered shawls for which Kirman has been renowned for hundreds of years, in fact since they were admired by Marco Polo who passed through Kirman on his travels in the 13th century.

The Chelsea carpet. Detail
Victoria and Albert Museum, Crown Copyright

These Kirman shawls may well have been the precursors of those made in Kashmir and Paisley, with which they are sometimes confused.

The Herati-mahi design perhaps matches the popularity of the pine-cone motif. This 'Herat-fish' pattern consisted originally of two fishes leaping round a central pool, but it is not seen in this form today. Specimens of the original pattern are rare. One example is in the Gulistan Palace where there is a large carpet on the floor of one room which shows this pattern with one fish above another, head to tail in parallel, closely covering the whole ground of the carpet. Today the fishes are replaced by two leaves spaced about a rosette. This is repeated on each side of a diamond-shaped centre and the whole design group is then repeated over and over again throughout the carpet. The border used with this design is almost invariably the 'turtle' or 'samovar' pattern. It is most popular with the weavers of Bijar whose carpets are amongst the strongest in Persia, so taut that one is well advised not to fold them inwards for fear of snapping the warp strands. A safer way is to roll the carpet with the pile outwards.

A design often used by Senneh weavers whose beautiful kilim-woven rugs are all too rarely made today, takes the form of a flower vase with two birds nestling in the flowers, or one bird hovering above the other feeding the second one on the nest. This is called the Gul-i bulbul design – the rose and the nightingale – and is also made in fine quality by the weavers of Qum.

Several Hamadan villages produce some rugs and runners with two or more medallions in series down the middle, against a camel and cream diaper patterned background. These are called 'Shir va Shakar' (milk and sugar) from which the word 'seersucker' is derived.

The Gul-i hena or henna flower pattern, three or four daisy-like flowers growing above one another in a straight line on either side of a straight central stem, sometimes with the same petalled flower at the top of the stem, was more often seen at the turn of the century than it is today. It was then a popular design for the closely-covered grounds of Mahal carpets made in Arak, where now the Sultanabad Saraband pine-cone pattern appears to be preferred.

The designs of carpets and rugs woven in the north are much more angular than are those of the villages of south or central Persia which have more rounded, softer-shaped motifs. Azarbaijan villages, especially those east of Tabriz in the long plain between the Savalan mountain range to the north and the Bazqush to the south, produce the Heriz and Georavan qualities. Their designs are most geometric. It is impossible to recognize a particular flower shape. Perhaps this is due as much to the strong Turkish orthodox influence as to the fact that the low number of knots to the square inch precludes any attempt at detail.

The subject of village rugs must not be left without mention of the products of Joshaqan in the lonely Varganeh mountains west and south of Kashan, some seventy miles north of Isfahan. Leaving aside the question as to whether it was here that, according to Upham Pope, the 'Polish' carpets were made 300 and more years ago, for many years now Joshaqan has only produced one design. This takes the form of a number of formally executed series of patterns spaced diagonally next to each other in row upon row about a central diamond-shaped medallion, inside which, as often as not, the design continues. This design only varies as to whether or not it is to include a medallion, and whether or not the medallion will or will not be balanced by corner pieces. When finely knotted, a Joshaqan carpet is very hand-some indeed with its rich red ground and star-like flowers.

It is in the bigger towns – Tabriz, Mashhad, Qum, Kashan, Arak, Yazd and Kirman – that one finds the finest specimens of the weavers' craft. To achieve their most intricate designs, town weavers must use loom-drawings which contain as many small squares as there are to be knots in the carpet. After the artist has drawn his design on this squared paper, he indicates to his assistants the general colourings desired and it is their task to paint each small square with the colour of the knot. The weaver, reading along the row of coloured squares, ties the knots accordingly.

Each town has developed its own distinctive style of colouring. A glance is usually enough for the expert to tell the difference between the glowing red velvet appear-ance of a medallion style Kashan with its strictly exact execution and the free-flowing delightfully soft-coloured Kirman carpet, showing likenesses of all types of flowers, particularly roses, carnations and daisies or human or animal figures – tiger, deer or hare. It is certainly not difficult to pick out either the Kashan or the Kirman types from the *Farsi-baf* (Persian-weave, to distinguish it from the alien recently introduced *Turki-baf*, Turkish-knotted) Mashhad carpet with its strongly coloured harder design.

The weavers of Qum deserve high praise for consistently maintaining a rare degree of excellence. They are particularly to be congratulated for their use of traditional designs. One finds little or no foreign influence here. Their rugs are thin and closely-knotted; pliable, but strong. Qum and Kashan rugs are perhaps the most dependable rugs in Persia today, and those from Nain the most closely knotted.

Tabriz is unquestionably the largest producing centre, outside influence being strong. Their carpets are made in all kinds of designs, many of which are not of Tabriz origin. Tabriz weavers are highly skilled and their work is accurate. Unlike other weavers they use a hook in making their knots. The best qualities are most closely woven. If a Tabriz carpet is woven in a Kirman design, it will have a more masculine appearance than its Kirman prototype.

A rewarding study could be made of the different uses of colour detail in each producing centre. The freest use of colour may be found in Kirman, even though it is here that the carpet colourist observes strict conventions or the typical nature of a Kirman carpet would be lost. Carpets made in the village of Ravar north of Kirman were famous at the turn of the century for their consistent excellence. To-day Yazd carpets seem likely to usurp Ravar's paramount position. Ravar must look to its laurels. Similarly Yazd weavers must watch that their colours do not become too hard. They should more closely follow the former Kirman conventions. A light blue carpet may have a border of cream or light rose. One seldom or never sees a Kirman carpet with a green ground or border. A flower in light pistachio green, with a darker pistachio shade used equally in the same flower, is typical of Kirman colouring. Each Kirman flower must be shaded by the use of two complementary tones of the same colour; but the choice of colours for the flower is strictly limited to those appropriate for use on the ground colour. Most important of all is the choice of the outline colour to be used round each petal or outside each stem to give definition to the pattern. This contrasting outline must itself be evenly balanced by the use of other complementary sets of shades in the general colouring of the carpet. The colouring must be precise, not blatant; it must give definition to the pattern, yet remain unobtrusive.

With all these rules and conventions to be observed consciously or unconsciously, how fortunate it is that Persians seem born with a draughtsman's skill and so gifted with an unerring sense of colour! It is for these gifts that we are grateful, for they bring us the joy of Persia's carpet heritage.